Ambrose / Harris

IMAGE

n. the optical appearance
of something produced in a
mirror or through a lens etc.

Academia
the environment of learning

AVA publishing SA
Switzerland

An AVA Book

Published by AVA Publishing SA

Rue des Fontenailles 16, Case postale

1000 Lausanne 6, Switzerland

Tel: +41 786 005 109 Email: enquiries@avabooks.ch

Distributed by Thames & Hudson (ex-North America)

181a High Holborn, London WC1V 7QX, United Kingdom

Tel: +44 20 7845 5000 Fax: +44 20 7845 5055

Email: sales@thameshudson.co.uk

www.thamesandhudson.com

For distribution in the USA and Canada please contact:

English Language Support Office

AVA Publishing (UK) Ltd.

Tel: + 44 1903 204 455 Email: sales@avabooks.co.uk

English Language Support Office

AVA Publishing (UK) Ltd.

Tel: +44 1903 204 455 Email: enquiries@avabooks.co.uk

Copyright © AVA Publishing SA 2005

All rights reserved. No part of this publication may be reproduced,
stored in a retrieval system or transmitted in any form or by any means,
electronic, mechanical, photocopying, recording or otherwise, without
permission of the copyright holder.

ISBN 2-88479-0659

10 9 8 7 6 5 4 3 2 1

Design and text by Gavin Ambrose and Paul Harris
with the assistance of Ashley Sansom
Original photography by Xavier Young
www.xavieryoung.co.uk
Original book and series concept devised by Natalia Price-Cabrera

Production and separations by AVA Book Production Pte. Ltd., Singapore
Tel: +65 6334 8173 Fax: +65 6334 0752 Email: production@avabooks.com.sg

Image

Client: This Is A Magazine
Design: Studio KA
Image description:
Photographs of cut-up
photographic portraits

This Is A Magazine

These two images were created by Studio KA for *This Is A Magazine* and feature photographic prints that have been cut into strips, curled at the bottom or curved entirely, and then photographed to produce surrealist results. This approach highlights one of the many ways that designers can turn a rather straightforward image – in this instance photographic portraits – into striking and interesting pieces of image manipulation.

Contents

Aboud Sodano

The Kitchen

Intro

Image Contents

Sagmeister Inc.

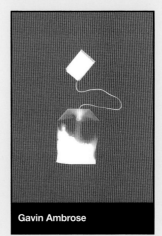

Gavin Ambrose

Lobo

Image Contents

Image refers to the graphic elements that can bring a design alive. Whether used for the main focus of a page or as a subsidiary element, images play an essential role in communicating a message and therefore form a key part in establishing the visual identity of a piece of work. Images perform a number of functions; from conveying the drama of a narrative to encapsulating and supporting an argument presented in the text, or simply providing a visual break to an expanse of copy or empty space. Images are effective because they provide detailed information, or invoke a feeling that the reader can comprehend very quickly. How would you describe the latest fashion trend in words? It would surely be more complex than the relative ease of conveying it in a picture.

Image usage is determined by many considerations, these include: what the desired impact is, who the target audience is, the aesthetic of the project, the function the image will serve and how adventurous or conservative the overall design needs to be. Image usage is perhaps the most exciting aspect of design because images can have a profound impact on the outcome and success of a piece of work due to the emotional reaction they can precipitate in the viewer. However, if images are poorly used they can detract from, or counteract, the message in the text. Within this book we explore some of the many techniques employed when using images and how they may subsequently be interpreted. A series of examples from contemporary design studios serve as testament to the enormous power of images.

The Basics

Before you begin to work with images an understanding of the basic terminology applied to them is required. This section introduces terms such as 'bitmap' and 'resolution' and explains why these terms are important.

Techniques

Images can be used to instil a range of emotional values and styles in a design. This section looks at how these values and styles can be enhanced by formatting choices and reproduction methods.

What Images Mean

Images contain 'coded' information that helps a viewer decide how they should receive and react to what they are viewing. Symbolic meanings may be communicated instantly. An awareness of semiotics allows us to understand why designers make the image choices that they do.

Using Images

Many techniques exist that enable a designer to optimise graphic usage within a design and enhance the impact that images have. These include: use of visual continuity, juxtaposition, vista and patterns.

Images in Practice

Photographs can communicate a message without further embellishment, but this section looks at the various image manipulation techniques available to a designer to change their appearance and the impact within a design.

Mark Making

Mark making ranges from simple representative lines to symbols, pictograms and ink blots. This section shows how made marks are versatile and particularly useful for conveying a set of emotional values to a viewer.

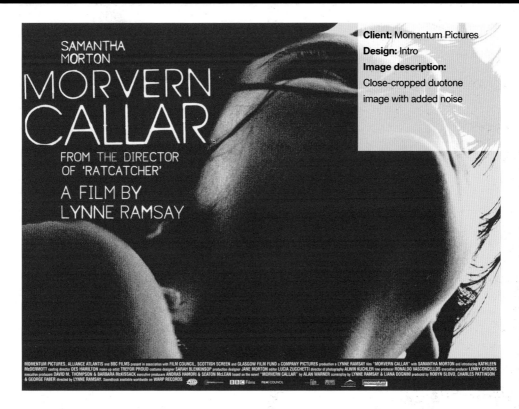

Client: Momentum Pictures
Design: Intro
Image description:
Close-cropped duotone
image with added noise

Morvern Callar

Intro design studio created this poster for the Lynne Ramsay film *Morvern Callar*.
The image features a red/yellow duotone (see page 24), with white typography.
The image provides information on two levels. Its denotive (see page 70) aspects
are what the viewer understands from the image itself and the cognitive aspects
are what we perceive from how it is presented. For instance, on a denotive level the
image is of a girl, but her upturned head with hair awry gives a cognitive perception
of vulnerability. The image has been reproduced with noise to add a gritty texture
and has also been close cropped to her head and shoulders to suggest a dramatic
snap-shot sense of immediacy. The low-grade quality of the image is intentional
and provides a visual reference that alludes to the gritty nature of the film.

Noise

In a visual context, noise describes an effect that produces random and unobtrusive degradation of image
quality. It is often used to replicate the grain of photographic film in order to give a gritty cast to an image. As
the grain of an image increases, so too does the noise.

Image Introduction

This book introduces different aspects of image design via dedicated chapters for each topic. Each chapter provides numerous examples of creative image use in design from leading contemporary design studios, annotated to explain the reasons behind the design choices made.

Key design principles are isolated so that the reader can see how they are applied in practice.

Clear navigation

Each chapter has a clear strapline to allow readers to quickly locate areas of interest.

Introductions

Special section introductions outline basic concepts that will be discussed.

Four-colour separation

20 **21**

Four-colour separation

A colour image is produced by separating the three trichromatic colours – cyan, magenta and yellow – and incorporating black; these form the process colours utilised in four-colour printing.

Nearly all colours can be printed using a combination of the subtractive primaries. The four-colour printing process uses separate printing plates – each containing its own subtractive primary – and layers these plates to build an image. A fourth black plate is incorporated to add depth to elements such as shadows.

Above (left to right): cyan, cyan + magenta, cyan + magenta + yellow, and finally the black plate is added.

If an image is built up with several colours it is possible to alter the image simply by altering one colour. In this row of images above (left to right); adding more black to the four-colour image makes it darker, adding cyan makes the image colder, adding yellow makes it warmer and reducing the magenta level lightens the reds in the image.

In this series the printing plates have been transposed, a mistake that sometimes occurs during the printing process. This means that the information intended for one channel or ink has been mistakenly used for another. This technique can sometimes be used deliberately to produce creative effects.

Image The Basics

Client: R. Newbold
Design: Aboud Sodano
Image description:
Four-colour separation used as a feature of the catalogue design

R. Newbold
This catalogue for fashion company R. Newbold was designed by Aboud Sodano and features a series of printed pages separated by a series of cyan, magenta, yellow and black prints. The images are printed on continuous feed dot-matrix printer paper; a low-cost stock. The substrate is very thin, and the pages are attached as a series of four-colour sets, similar to the printing film that would be sent to the printer to create a four-colour publication.

Image Four-colour separation

Written explanations

Key points are explained within the context of an example project.

Examples

Commercial projects from contemporary designers bring the principles under discussion alive.

Diagrams

Diagrams add meaning to theory by showing the basic principles in action.

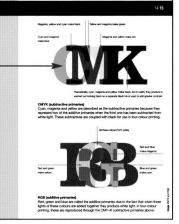

Additional information

Clients, designers and image descriptions are included.

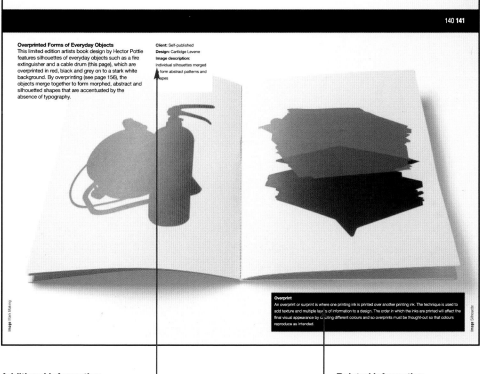

Related information

Related information such as definitions are isolated and explained.

Image How to get the most out of this book

Client: This Is A Magazine
Design: Studio KA
Image description:
Image pared back to key
elements, but still retaining a
sense of expression

The Basics

The production of images for publications, packaging and other uses is now widely achieved through the use of computer technology. A designer needs to be aware of many considerations when producing an image. These might include the resolution – the amount of data or information that an electronic image contains – required for the image to reproduce at the optimum quality, or the format to be used, as different image types are stored in different file formats. Photorealistic images, for example, are commonly stored in a bitmap file format, while logo artwork and line drawings are generally stored in an EPS (Encapsulated PostScript) file. This chapter will introduce some of the common terms and basic concepts behind image reproduction.

Pictures are used in designs for a wide variety of reasons, they might provide an example or illustration of the subject matter under discussion, or they may be used to convey a message. Images can be used to invoke a range of emotions and responses in the viewer for example, an image of a much-loved sports star in close proximity to a product may suggest the celebrity is endorsing it. Images can convey ideas very quickly, much quicker than if they were described in text, and because of this they form a key weapon in a designer's armoury.

Kiss and Make Up (left)
This image is a reductive representation of the face of rock legend Alice Cooper, which was produced by Studio KA as part of a series of images for *This Is A Magazine*. The key elements of this image, such as the mouth and eyes, have been pared back to a basic form that retains and emphasises their expressive qualities.

Resolution

The resolution value of an image refers to how much information it contains and therefore the level of detail that it has. The higher the resolution value, the more information the image contains.

With more information, and therefore a higher resolution value, the better the quality of the reproduction. Higher resolution also means that the image can be reproduced at a larger scale without noticeably showing loss of information or quality. The terms DPI and PPI are commonly confused. Although DPI has become a generic term to describe image resolution, it refers exclusively to the image in printed format. PPI is a digital image representation and is less 'physical' than DPI.

DPI (dots per inch) measures how many ink dots a printer can deposit within an inch. For printing purposes, a resolution of 300 DPI is standard.

PPI (pixels per inch) describes the number of pixels, displayed both horizontally and vertically, in each square inch of a digital image.

LPI (lines per inch) value derives from the way that printers reproduce photographic images. Photographs are reproduced as a series of halftone dots of different sizes. The larger the dots, the darker the image produced and vice versa. To produce halftone dots a printer uses a halftone grid, which is divided into cells. The LPI value is a measurement of how close these cells are to each other. With a low LPI value there are fewer cells, and the halftone dots will be more obvious in the printed image. Only highly absorbent paper can reproduce low LPI images due to the ink spread.

Pixelation occurs where the resolution of an image is too low for printing. Pixels are large and coarse-looking and will compromise any detail in the image. Increasing the size of a low-resolution image only spreads the original pixel information over a greater area and will result in severe pixelation.

Artifacts

Artifacts, or blotches, can occur in images saved as JPEG files that have been compressed too much. Artifacts may make it seem that there is colour leakage at the edge of objects.

If you resize an image you will add to or subtract from the amount of information it contains. For example, if you double the resolution of an image from 150 LPI to 300 LPI you will also double the size of the image that is produced. Simply increasing the resolution will proportionally improve the quality of an image because the amount of improvement that is possible will depend upon the amount of information contained in the original image, be it electronic or print. An image produced from 35mm film cannot be reproduced as large as a 10 x 8 inch transparency without losing quality, as this requires more information than the 35mm film ever contained. If an image needs to be reproduced at a larger size without loss of quality it will need to be scanned again, reprinted, or in extreme cases photographed again.

Interpolation tries to address this by resampling the information in the image. Interpolation seeks to change the image by adding in new information that is estimated by taking an average of known values at neighbouring points in the image.

300 PPI

This image is the correct resolution for printing.

200 PPI

Visible pixelation starts to occur as the resolution is reduced.

150 PPI

Pixelation continues as resolution is further reduced.

  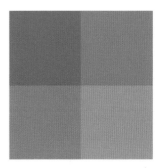

100 PPI

With further reduction, the pixels continue to increase in size...

50 PPI

... until the image appears to be very crude.

2 PPI

Finally, only coloured blocks remain and the recognisable image is lost.

Image Resolution

CMYK and RGB

Information about an image's colour is stored either as CMYK (cyan, magenta, yellow and black) or RGB (red, green and blue). The difference between the two is the colour separation process used.

Offset lithographic printing is a four-colour process that combines cyan, magenta and yellow printing inks (the subtractive primaries), with black to reproduce red, green and blue (the additive primaries), as shown in the diagram opposite. When combined, red, green and blue lights produce white light, which is why they are called additive primaries. The eye contains receptors that react to the additive colours to form the images that we see.

Designers will usually create a piece of work on screen using the additive RGB colours because the file size is smaller and more manageable. However, to reproduce a colour image, a process of colour separation is needed (see below), so that printing plates can be produced that will recreate the additive colours of a design, photograph or artwork. For this purpose, files are saved with CMYK colours so that they contain all the information required for four-colour printing.

Colour separation

Colour separation describes the relationship between the additive primaries that we see, and the subtractive primaries that are used for printing. Filters of red, green and blue (the additive colours), are used to produce separation negatives. The red filter allows only the blue and green components through and so creates cyan. The blue filter allows red and green through to create yellow and the green filter lets through red and blue, which creates magenta. Each negative produces a positive, which is then used to make plates to be printed in sequence (yellow, magenta, cyan). Due to the limitations of printing ink, black is also added to ensure good contrast and shadow reproduction.

Colour space

Colour space is a means of specifying the requirements of a colour such as HSL (Hue, Saturation and Lightness), HSI (Hue, Saturation and Intensity), and HSV (Hue, Saturation and Value). RGB and CMYK are the standard colour spaces used for online and printing purposes respectively. Within RGB and CMYK models there are a series of specific colour spaces that are matched to regional outputs. For example, the colour information of an image can be altered depending on where it is being printed – US, Europe or Japan. Controlling the colour space will ensure accurate viewing and proofing of an image's colour properties. It is important to know the colour space that a printer requires files to be supplied in, as this is necessary for maintaining colour accuracy when the job is printed.

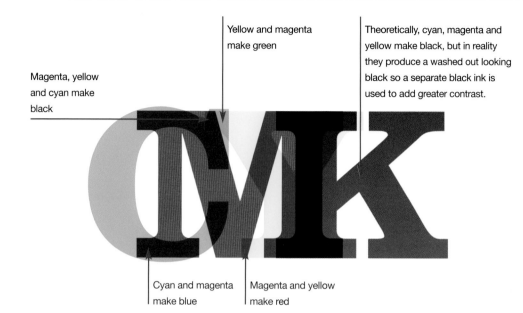

Magenta, yellow and cyan make black

Yellow and magenta make green

Theoretically, cyan, magenta and yellow make black, but in reality they produce a washed out looking black so a separate black ink is used to add greater contrast.

Cyan and magenta make blue

Magenta and yellow make red

CMYK (subtractive primaries)

Cyan, magenta and yellow are described as the subtractive primaries because they represent two of the additive primaries when the third one has been subtracted from white light. These subtractives are coupled with black for use in four-colour printing.

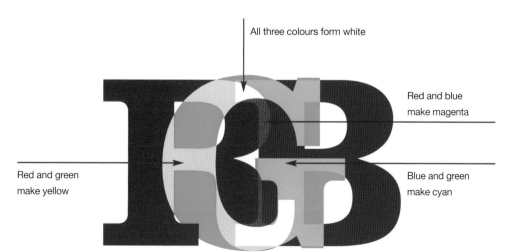

All three colours form white

Red and blue make magenta

Red and green make yellow

Blue and green make cyan

RGB (additive primaries)

Red, green and blue are called the additive primaries due to the fact that when three lights of these colours are added together they produce white light. In four-colour printing, these are reproduced through the CMY+K subtractive primaries above.

Image CMYK and RGB

Bitmaps and vectors

There are essentially two types of image formats: bitmaps (or photographic) and vectors (or line art). Both formats have specific strengths and weaknesses that make them suitable for different purposes.

A bitmap, or raster, is any image that is composed of pixels in a grid. Each pixel contains colour information for the reproduction of the image. Bitmap graphics are not usually scalable because they have a fixed resolution, which means that should you resize the image it will become distorted and have a jagged, pixelated edge. Bitmaps are especially good if used for the reproduction of detailed, tonal imagery, like the subtle tones seen in the image below.

A vector image contains many individual, scalable objects that are defined by mathematical formulae rather than pixels. A vector graphic is therefore scalable or resolution independent, for example, fonts are vector objects. The main disadvantage of vector images is that they are unsuitable for reproducing photorealistic images because they cannot depict the continuous subtle tones of a photograph.

Bitmap image at 100%

Vector image at 100%

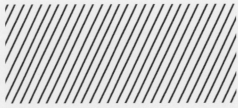

Enlargement at 1000%

When reproduced at 100% tonal graduations can be clearly seen in the bitmap, but at 1000% the individual pixels can be seen and the graduation lost.

Enlargement at 1000%

A vector image is not constructed with pixels and so it remains clear even when enlarged by 1000%.

Client: Zanders Papers
Design: Research Studios
Image description:
Combining the tonal qualities
of bitmap with the sharp line
reproduction of a vector.

Zanders Papers
This promotional poster combines bitmap (photographic) and vector (line art)
elements to create the final image shown here. By layering these two image formats
together the designers have added depth to the image.

Working with bitmaps

As previously discussed, bitmaps are essentially very simple monotone graphic elements. This enables the colour characteristics of elements to be controlled independently of the original image.

The six images below, for example, are all rendered from the same original source file: a single black and white image. All the colour information is applied independently from the image, while the original colour characteristics of the source file remain preserved.

Areas of an image can be directly filled with colour, or a panel of colour can be positioned so that it appears in a particular section of the image. The six examples below print in silver, yellow, a gradient between the two, magenta, cyan and a graduated black. In the opposite spread, a series of bitmaps have been overprinted in graduating tones to create a graphic effect.

Working with a bitmap file is relatively straightforward if you bear in mind what the limitations of the format are, namely that it is a scale-dependent format and cannot be resized without potentially distorting the image.

Image The Basics

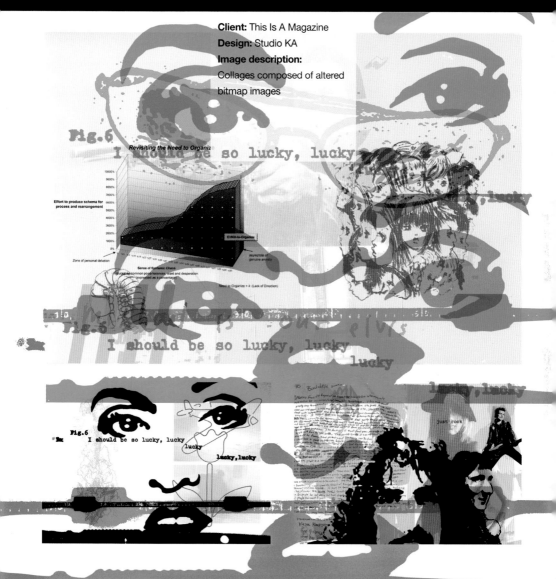

Client: This Is A Magazine
Design: Studio KA
Image description:
Collages composed of altered
bitmap images

This Is A Magazine

These spreads were created by Studio KA design studio for *This Is A Magazine*. They feature various collages that relate to pop music and are composed of bitmap images that have been overlaid to build a dynamic and colourful composite image. When overlaying images you can 'knockout' or 'overprint' (see page 156); each of these methods create very different effects.

Gradient

A gradient is a colour fill that increases in intensity from nothing through various tonal gradations to solid colour, or from one colour to another.

Image Working with bitmaps

Four-colour separation

A colour image is produced by separating the three trichromatic colours – cyan, magenta and yellow – and incorporating black; these form the process colours utilised in four-colour printing.

Nearly all colours can be printed using a combination of the subtractive primaries. The four-colour printing process uses separate printing plates – each containing its own subtractive primary – and layers these plates to build an image. A fourth black plate is incorporated to add depth to elements such as shadows.

Above (left to right): cyan, cyan + magenta, cyan + magenta + yellow, and finally the black plate is added.

If an image is built up with several colours it is possible to alter the image simply by altering one colour. In this row of images (left to right): adding more black to the four-colour image makes it darker; adding cyan makes the image colder; adding yellow makes it warmer and reducing the magenta level lightens the reds in the image.

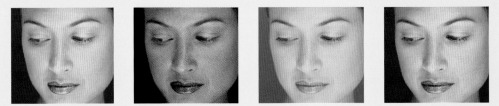

In this series the printing plates have been transposed, a mistake that sometimes occurs during the printing process. This means that the information intended for one channel or ink has been mistakenly used for another. This technique can sometimes be used deliberately to produce creative effects.

Client: R. Newbold
Design: Aboud Sodano
Image description:
Four-colour separation used
as a feature of the catalogue
design

R. Newbold

This catalogue for fashion company R. Newbold was designed by Aboud Sodano and features a series of printed pages accompanied by a series of cyan, magenta, yellow and black prints. The images are printed on continuous feed dot-matrix printer paper; a low-cost stock. The substrate is very thin, and the pages are attached as a series of four-colour sets, similar to the film that would be sent to a printer in order to create a four-colour publication.

Image Four-colour separation

Special colours

The four-colour printing process can reproduce a wide array of colours, but it is far from exhaustive. To produce certain colours in a design the use of a special colour is required. This 'special' is applied via a fifth printing plate.

A special colour is a solid colour and not one that is made up of dots, as is the case with four-colour printing. A special colour cannot be made using the CMYK process colours and might be a metallic, fluorescent, pastel or Pantone (PMS) ink.

As a special colour has a particular hue and saturation that is not possible to achieve by the standard four-colour process, it can be a way to introduce fuller and richer colours to a design (as can be seen below). This book prints in six colours: the standard four-process colours and three special colours. In addition to this spread, the special colours appear on pages 18–19, 26–27, and 30–31.

CMYK
These are the standard process colours used in four-colour printing.

Special colours
Special colours can lift a design because they are brighter and more vibrant than combinations of the process colours.

The square on the left is special colour Pantone 806, while the one on the right is the same colour produced using the standard four-colour process. Notice how much brighter and resonant the special colour appears.

The same is true for metallic colours. The left square is a metallic silver special that has a vibrancy that is not replicable by the four-colour process, which produces a square (right) that appears grey.

Image The Basics

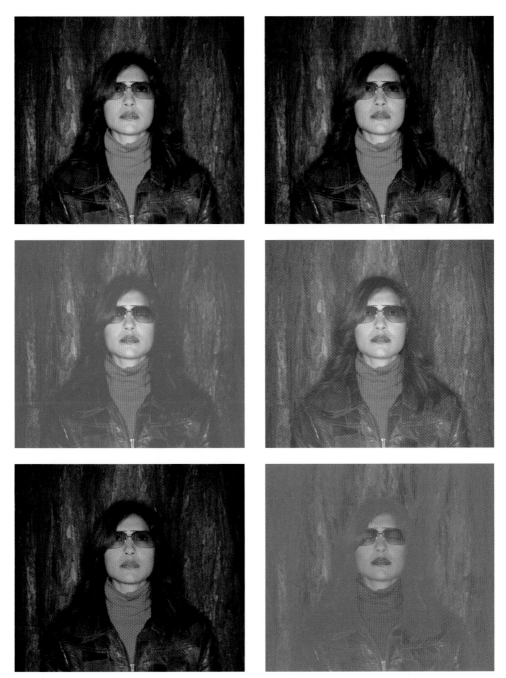

Clockwise from top left: a four-colour image with a graduated tint of Pantone 806; a four-colour image with a graduated tint of Pantone 877; a black plate printing as Pantone 806; an image with a base layer of Pantone 806; an image with a base layer of Pantone 877 and a black plate printing as Pantone 877.

Image Special colours

Duotones, tritones and quadtones

Tonal images may be produced using black and one of the other subtractive primaries. In essence, a tonal image is akin to a black-and-white photograph in which the white tones have been replaced by one, or a combination, of the other process colours. Duotones use two tones, tritones use three tones and quadtones use four tones.

The use of tones helps create a level playing field between images particularly where they have different qualities such as greyscale and colour, or have originated from different sources such as archive or stock. Colour detail can be reduced to two, three or four tones as shown below.

Duotones

A duotone uses two tones, typically black and one other process colour.

Tritones

A tritone uses three tones, typically black and two other process colours. The use of two more tones in addition to black can create a warmer feel to the lighter areas of the image.

Quadtones

Quadtones use four tones, typically black and the three other process colours. This produces a black and white image with greater contrast and shadow depth.

Duotone of yellow and black.

Tritone of yellow, black and magenta.

Quadtone of yellow, black, magenta and cyan.

Image The Basics

Client: Transworld
Design: Research Studios
Image description:
Duotone breaker pages, each
using a different colour

Transworld

Shown here is a series of breaker pages, which were taken from a catalogue produced by Research Studios for publishing house Transworld. Each breaker page features a semi-abstract duotone image of a book and each duotone is created with a different colour. The duotones retain detail in the image whilst producing a flat, even background colour. Had the backgrounds contained any black they would have appeared dull and muddied. The sparseness of the breaker pages provides a distinct separation between the publisher's different imprints, and yet retains an overall visual continuity.

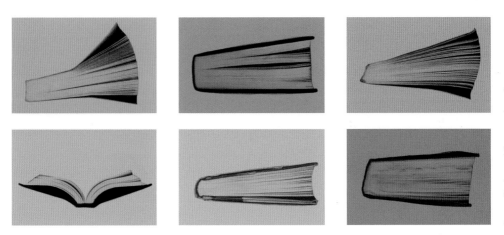

Image Duotones, tritones and quadtones

Controlling tonal images
Adjusting the channels on a tonal image can produce spectacular graphic effects as the images on this spread demonstrate. Adjustments are made by altering the image controls (see pages 28–29) on the respective colour curves.

This image is converted to greyscale (i.e. it prints on the black plate only).

A duotone image composed of yellow and black in equal proportions.

A duotone image composed of black and a high yellow saturation.

A duotone image composed of black and a high saturation of Pantone 806.

A duotone image composed of Pantone 806 and silver in equal proportions.

A duotone image composed of black and high saturation of silver.

Image The Basics

A duotone image composed of black and a high yellow saturation, with a reversal in the black plate curve.

A duotone image composed of magenta and Pantone 806 in equal proportions.

A duotone image composed of yellow and cyan.

A duotone image of yellow and magenta in equal proportions.

A duotone image composed of yellow and a high saturation of magenta.

A duotone image composed of magenta and cyan in equal proportions.

A tritone image composed of black, cyan and silver.

A quadtone that uses CMYK inks to give a warmer image.

A quadtone image composed of black, yellow, silver and Pantone 806.

Image controls

The colour information in an image can be controlled and altered in several different ways. Adjusting these controls does not change the material structure of the image (i.e. where the lines or image elements are), but the colour of these elements. These can be adjusted for corrective purposes, to obtain more lifelike colouration, or to produce graphic effects.

Saturation
The colour spectrum ranges from neutral grey to an array of bright colours, and saturation refers to any given colour's position within that range. Saturation is a measure of strength, purity or the amount of grey in relation to the hue.

Hue
The hue is the colour that is reflected or transmitted from an object. Hue is expressed as a value (between 0 and 360), on the colour wheel. An image can be altered by moving around the axis of the colour wheel. Changing hue values dramatically alters the colour of an image.

Brightness
The brightness refers to the amount of light used to produce a colour. The more light used, the brighter the colour. However, as one moves towards the maximum and minimum levels, the contrast value diminishes and so a mid-level that provides good contrast is preferred.

Contrast
Contrast is the difference between the highlights and the shadows of an image.

Gradient
The gradient allows specific colours to be applied to an image in order to create a graphic effect. Replacing all colours with silvery grey values for example creates a 'chromed' image.

Saturation left to right: normal image, red saturated, reduced red, all saturated, all reduced and blue saturated.

Hue left to right: this strip shows reducing values of the magenta hue. The normal image is shown third from left.

Brightness left to right: this strip shows increasing values of brightness. The normal image is shown third from left.

Contrast left to right: this strip shows increasing contrast values. The normal image is shown third from left.

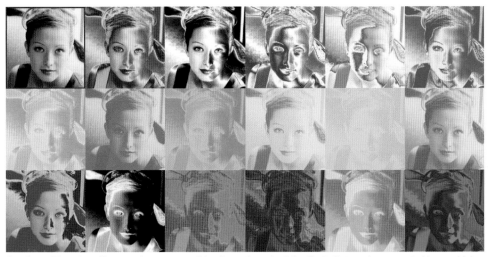

Gradient: this series of images shows some of the dramatic and subtle effects that can be generated by combining changes in the image controls. Alterations to the gradient values are shown in the images on the bottom row.

Channels

RGB images have three channels: red, green and blue. CMYK images have four: cyan, magenta, yellow and black, and contain the colour information used to produce plates for the four-colour printing process. The cyan channel, for example, is actually greyscale information that prints, or is displayed as, cyan. As each colour is a separate channel they can be independently altered, replaced or omitted.

Changing channels

The ability to manipulate the different colour channels allows a designer to make the necessary adjustments to obtain good colour balance, keeping in mind that during the printing process each colour usually prints (overprints) the same order; cyan, magenta, yellow and black. Adjusting the colour channels can be used to create dramatic or subtle changes to an image, as can be seen below and opposite.

The normal CMYK image as photographed.

Here the channels are adjusted to make the image subtly 'cooler'.

Here the channels are changed so that the yellow plate prints as silver.

Image The Basics

This image only uses the black channel.

Here the image is altered to print black on a Pantone 806 base.

Here the channels are altered to print black on silver.

This image has had the yellow channel omitted.

This image has been altered to contain more red tones.

This image has been altered to contain more green tones.

This image contains only black and cyan channels.

This image has an exaggerated yellow channel.

This image has an exaggerated cyan channel.

Client: British Council
Design: Pentagram
(Angus Hyland)
Image description:
Informal illustration combining
characteristics of both the
subject and potential viewer

CARACAS
EXPOSICIÓN
7 JUNIO - 28 JULIO
MUSEO DE ARTE CONTEMPORÁNEO
DE CARACAS SOFIA IMBER

BOGOTÁ
EXPOSICIÓN
15 AGOSTO - 7 SEPTIEMBRE
SALA DE ARTE ALBERTO URDANETA
BIBLIOTECA LUIS ÁNGEL ARANGO
BANCO DE LA REPÚBLICA

SANTIAGO DE CHILE
EXPOSICIÓN
25 SEPTIEMBRE - 10 OCTUBRE
GALERÍA DE ARTE CENTRO DE
EXTENSIÓN DE LA PONTIFICIA
UNIVERSIDAD CATÓLICA DE CHILE

PICTURE THIS
EN LATINOAMÉRICA
ILLUSTRACIÓN CONTEMPORÁNEA BRITÁNICA

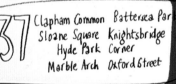

Techniques

Different image types and techniques are used and applied by designers to enhance the graphic elements in their design. Initially, the selection will focus on image type, such as the integration of a photograph, piece of line art or an illustration. The designer's decision then turns to what technique should be applied to the image type, such as silk screening, lithographic printing, sgraffito or die cutting. The format used will depend upon what method best conveys the intended message. Any method can be used to convey a particular idea, but each method will alter the presentation. For example both a photograph and an illustration of the Giza pyramids is likely to make the viewer think of Egypt. However, the illustration could have a photographic level of detailing or it could be more abstract, only capturing the vital essence of the pyramids – thus the type of image and the technique used to present it will undoubtedly influence the message communicated to the viewer.

This section covers the main techniques used for both creating images and reproducing them. Some reproduction methods maintain consistent standards between images while others do not, and so add a touch of individuality. For example, lithographic reproduction maintains accuracy while silk screening provides unique characteristics. Formatting choices can also add to the impact of an image, these choices may include the colour and texture of paper stock or the use of die cuts and other print finishing techniques.

Picture This (left)

For this poster, designed to promote the Latin American leg of the *Picture This* touring exhibition, Angus Hyland of Pentagram used an illustration of popular London imagery by Marion Deuchars. The familiar, almost stereotypical, London postcard icons (a red open-top bus and the statue of Eros in Piccadilly Circus), hint at the origin of the 17 contemporary London-based illustrators that are featured in the exhibition. The style of the illustration is simple and low key, which engenders a familiar, warm and approachable feel. The power of illustration is best seen in its ability to shape the content to incorporate characteristics of both the subject matter and the viewer. Hand drawn and stencilled typography further suggest the tone and content of the show.

Silk screening

Silk screening is a printing technique whereby ink is passed through a screen, which contains an image, and on to a substrate. The name comes from the silk that was originally used to support the stencil, or screen, carrying the image; nowadays a synthetic gauze or metal mesh is used instead. Silk screening can be used on virtually any surface. It provides a tactile element to a design and has its own visual aesthetic.

The silk-screen technique is not restricted to the four-process colours of offset lithography and is often used to apply special colours to a design, such as the black-and-white bitmap images that can be seen in the example opposite. Effectively, the silk screen is used to colour certain elements of the design, and this is performed so that the translucency of the printing inks used is such that it allows the black elements to show through.

The quality of silk screen printing is affected by two factors: mesh count and mesh grade.

Mesh count
Mesh count refers to the number of threads per inch. The lower the count the less support there is for detail and the heavier the deposit of ink.

Mesh grade
Mesh grade refers to the thickness of the thread, which influences the weight of the ink film. There are four grades: S (thin), M (somewhere between thin and normal), T (normal) HD (heavy duty or thick). The S grade provides a 50–70% open area and HD grade provides a 20–35% open area.

Client: Levi's
Design: The Kitchen
Image description:
Silk-screen printing over
bitmap images

Levi's

Clothing brands develop an image for their products so that they appeal to consumers. These in-store display panels, designed by The Kitchen for Levi's, convey a rough, urban, street-smart edge – an effect greatly enhanced by the production of the pieces.

Kate Gibb, who has produced work for clients such as the Chemical Brothers, was commissioned to make these silk-screen prints. The images of the models were made on previously used screens and this lent an extra layer of texture to the resulting work, which sees the models highlighted in colour against a toned background. Gibb created six unique images, each of which was displayed in Levi's flagship stores.

Levi's has long been at the forefront of branding and image creation and this extends to a tradition of using known artists, designers and illustrators, which includes another great silk-screen printer, Andy Warhol.

Image Silk screening

Illustration

For many designers, photography has superceded the medium of illustration – largely due to its ability to show detail within an image. However, the saturation of photographic images in printed media has caused some designers to return to illustration in order to create something distinct. An illustration can pass beyond the physical boundaries of a photographed object and thus, can emote and elucidate ideas in a way that a photograph cannot.

An illustration can convey the feeling of something very personal. This is largely due to the time an illustrator may take in order to create the image, and the fact that it is created by hand rather than through use of a mechanical device (although this is not always the case). The illustrations shown here replicate design sketches and as such, project the sensuality of the underwear without the distraction of photographic detail.

Image Techniques

Paul Smith

UNDERWEAR

2

Client: Paul Smith
Design: Aboud Sodano
Image description:
Delicate illustrations on
textured cartridge paper to
establish a sensual connection

Paul Smith Underwear

This brochure for a Paul Smith line of lingerie and swimwear was designed by Aboud
Sodano. It features images that have been delicately printed on to textured cartridge
paper to mimic the original water colour illustrations by Izak. The illustrations are used
to establish a sensual connection to the underwear, rather than just representing it
pictorially as a photograph would. The illustrations are delicate and fine, values that
by association, we apply to the garments portrayed.

Image Illustration

Client: Nike

Design: KesselsKramer

Image description:
Stylistic illustrations with grass effect

Or is it watch the ball,
and reach back for the strength of 400 747's?
An Instinct. Command. Reflex.
A Blink.
The forehand swing that
has been made 5,000,027 times before.
Maybe more.
Who's counting?
The glide of the slide as the tennis ball
spins like spaghetti over the net,
into the court,
and into the mighty green chorus of Wimbledon screams.

The Forehand

Nike

This booklet about the Wimbledon tennis tournament was created by KesselsKramer design studio for sporting goods manufacturer Nike. It features a series of poetic textual explanations for different tennis shots such as forehand and volley, and these are accompanied by stylistic sketches of the shots being performed. The illustrations have a grass-like visual quality that creates an obvious link to the fact that Wimbledon is a grass court competition.

Client: Ufi
Design: Iris Associates
Image description:
Painted portraits used to
enforce uniqueness and
style continuity

Ufi Strategic Plan 2002

Iris Associates design studio illustrated the case studies contained in the
Ufi/Learndirect strategic plan publication with portraits of the individuals they
featured. Rather than use photography the studio commissioned these painted
portraits in order to enforce a uniqueness to the publication. In addition to being a
break from the photographic norm, they ensured an inherent stylistic continuity
among them.

Image Illustration

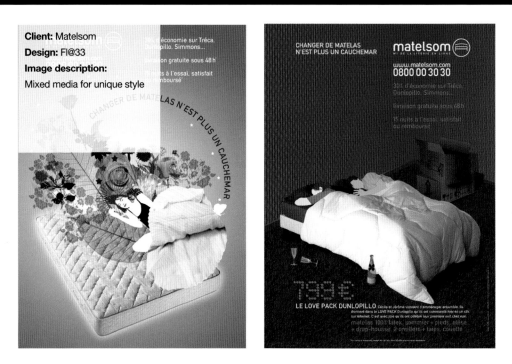

Client: Matelsom

Design: Fl@33

Image description:
Mixed media for unique style

Matelsom

This is a series of mixed-media promotional designs, which Fl@33 design studio produced for a print and online marketing campaign by Matelsom – a French e-commerce, furniture supplier. The mixed-media technique allows designers to exercise total control over photorealistic images and drawn elements in order to achieve a very stylish result. The examples shown demonstrate the variety of mixed-media illustrations that were used for advertisements, A4 envelopes and other communication pieces.

Client: Mother
Design: Intro
Image description:
Duotone composite images
that are shaped to form
numerals

Mother / Orange

Advertising agency Mother approached a number of design studios to create images for the 'Orange Numbers' campaign on behalf of mobile telephone company Orange. This particular design by Intro features composite images that are shaped to form the number '2000', which linked to an Orange promotion that gave new subscribers 2,000 free text messages.

The orange duotone used for the greater part of the image aids the production of the composite images by establishing colour equality. The colour serves as an integral part of the brand. The imagery created within the numerals is almost psychedelic and the numerals are styled as a typeface that is popularly associated with the late 1960s.

Psychedelic

Psychedelic refers to the vivid colours and bizarre patterns that are associated with psychedelic states, such as the distorted sensory perceptions obtained by ingesting psychedelic drugs. Psychedelia became a strong creative force in the late 1960s, which encompassed art, music, graphic design and literature as the younger generation sought to break with established societal conventions.

Image Illustration

Client: Franco Dessi

Design: Studio KA

Image description:

Pencil illustrations with
detailing in scientific style

D E S S

Spring and Summer 20

ixury Leatherbag Collect

Image Techniques

Dessi

This promotional catalogue for a collection of luxury leather bags was produced by
Studio KA for Franco Dessi. The brochure contains a series of pencil sketches on
cartridge paper in which only certain details have been completed and coloured. The
style is reminiscent of nineteenth century naturalist and scientific sketches, implying
that the illustrator has discovered unique and unusual specimens that have to be
recorded. Illustrations of the bags are juxtaposed with drawings of fauna and flora to
reinforce this concept, which also adds to the overall 'field guide' feel of the
publication.

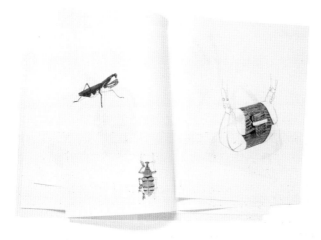

Pencil illustrations of bag designs are interspersed with those of flora and fauna in the Dessi catalogue. Areas of detail are highlighted in colour to command the full attention of the viewer.

Image Illustration

Client: SVB
Design:
Faydherbe / De Vringer
Image description:
Archive photos and illustrations
used for centenary annual
report

SVB Annual Report

Social security bank SVB, celebrated its 100th anniversary in 2000. To coincide with these celebrations, Faydherbe / De Vringer decided to trawl through SVB's archives to source the images that form an integral part of this design. The images and illustrations they used add an historical touch to the report, which is in keeping with the centenary celebrations.

Image Techniques

Client: Q 101

Design: Segura Inc.

Image description:

Comic-book style illustrations,

used in an unexpected context

Q 101

Images can be misleading as the designs shown above demonstrate. What at first appears to be a selection of cover illustrations for a series of comic books turns out to be a series of promotional images for a number of rock bands – each 'comic book' is dedicated to a different group. The comic-book images by Segura Inc. design studio are far removed from how we are accustomed to receiving information about rock music, and demonstrate both a potential benefit and disadvantage of using specific genres or types of image outside of their designated or anticipated context.

Image Illustration

Photography

Photography is now a mainstay for image-based content. This is due to its ability to provide a high level of information and convey a range of emotions, as well as its relative cheapness (especially with digital cameras), and ease of manipulation via computer programs to produce a variety of resulting effects. Photographs are typically stored as digital files in PSD, TIFF or JPEG formats.

PSD (PhotoShop Document) is a file format that supports all available image modes (bitmap, greyscale, duotone, RGB, CMYK and so on). This versatility means it is widely used by designers while they are working on an image, but its incompatibility with other applications means a completed image is usually converted to a TIFF or JPEG format.

TIFF (Tagged Image File Format) is a flexible method for storing halftones or colour bitmap images. They are cross-platform compatible and retain better image quality than JPEG files and as such are more suitable for printing.

JPEG (Joint Photographic Experts Group) is a file format that contains 24-bit colour information (i.e. 6.7 million colours), and uses compression to discard image information. It is suitable for those images with complex pixel gradations in continuous tone such as photographs. As the JPEG format compresses file size, image quality may suffer when printed unless maximum quality settings are selected and the resolution is at least 300 DPI.

Image Techniques

Client: Bailhache Labesse
Design: HGVFelton
Image description:
Full-face portraits displayed on short-cut breaker pages that combine to create a composite face

A Different Face

This is an annual review produced for Jersey law firm Bailhache Labesse by HGVFelton design studio. The publication focuses on the staff of the practice and incorporates full-face portrait photographs of eight people that work there as breaker pages, which personalises the document and also suggests that the firm provides personal service. From the back, each section that is broken by a portrait page is cut progressively shorter so that they combine to form a cover, which reveals another face constructed from strips of each of the different portrait photographs.

Image Photography

Client: Citigroup Private Bank
Design: North
Image description: Realist
and reportage photography

The Citigroup Private Bank Photography Prize 2002

This spread features pages from the exhibition catalogue that supported the Citigroup Private Bank Photography Prize in 2002. The catalogue was created by North design studio and features striking realist and reportage photography that celebrates ordinary people in their own environments. The use of a neutral sans-serif typeface and the physical separation of image and text pages allows the viewer's attention to remain focused on the photographs.

The spreads featured here demonstrate the simple presentation of the photography. The almost full-page images have a dramatic quality because of their scale relative to the size of the publication. This sense of scale is further enhanced by effects such as passe partout framing and single-edge bleeds that provide an entrance point to an image. By juxtaposing each image with a blank page the feelings of isolation and distress, which we feel coming from the subject of the photograph, are enhanced (right).

The ability of photography to convey strong emotions is heightened by the image's presentation at near full-page scale. This provides a more engaging level of detail for the viewer, who is compelled to focus on the stark presentation of facial expressions (left).

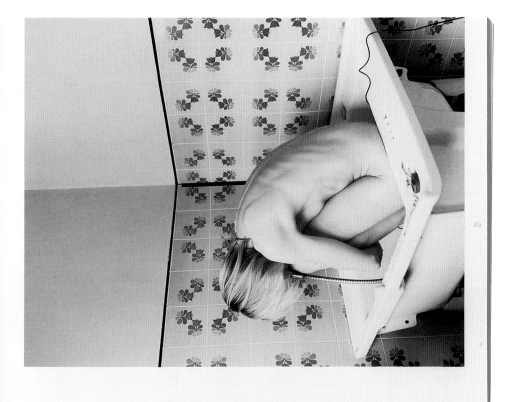

49

Client: Pathé
Design: Research Studios
Image description:
Muted tones drain the reassuring glance of the character, who is knowingly heading towards her death

THE VIRGIN SUICIDES

James Woods
Kathleen Turner
Kirsten Dunst
Hanna Hall
Chelse Swain
Leslie Hayman
Danny DeVito

a film by Sofia Coppola

Director/Writer Sofia Coppola Executive Producer Fred Fuchs Executive Producer Willi Baer Co-Producer Fred Roos
Co-Producer Gary Marcus Producer Francis Ford Coppola Producer Julie Constanzo Producer Dan Halsted
Producer Chris Hanley DOP Edward Lachman Editor James Lyons Production Designer Jasna Stefanovic
Costume Designer Nancy Steiner Assitant to the producer Tarek Khan

The Virgin Suicides

This poster was designed by Research Studios to promote the film *The Virgin Suicides*. In the photograph, Kirsten Dunst appears to be walking into the sun towards her future and death, but she has stopped to look over her shoulder at the viewer. The glance she gives and the smile on her face suggest a certain reassurance that she knows what she is doing, although the muted tones of the image hint at the life that will soon be ebbing away.

Client: Toi Com Moi
Design: FI@33
Image description:
Photographs of family scenes, which are spliced to suggest a sense of movement.

Toi Com Moi

These images are part of an advertising campaign created by FI@33 for Parisian fashion label Toi Com Moi. The label designs clothing for parents and children so that fathers and sons, and mothers and daughters can purchase items that match. The designs feature photographs of domestic life. The reportage images are spliced together to give a feeling of movement, much like that of a home movie, a device often used in cinema to suggest idyllic childhood days.

Image Photography

Filters

Whether attached to a camera or applied to a digital image, a filter is used to filter light of specific wavelengths in order to change the presentation of the final image.

Filters are used to make subtle adjustments to an image such that the viewer is often unaware that any manipulation has taken place, for example, refining a colour image to create an opal-blue sky or a coral-sand beach. They are also used to make more dramatic and graphic interventions.

These images (above) of a beach sunset have been produced with different filters. Top row, left to right: the original image, increased shadows and deeper shadows. Middle row, left to right: tonal balancing, mid-tone emphasis and highlight emphasis. Bottom row, left to right: the image with a red cast, yellow cast and a blue cast. Subtle adjustments have been made to images in the first two rows and more dramatic changes in the last.

This Is A Magazine (right)

This illustration was created by Studio KA for *This Is A Magazine,* and was created by overlaying two images. The photograph of the nude woman is overlaid with a photograph of a tie-die pattern that partially clothes her. In many contemporary designs this process is achieved electronically, but in the past the effect would have been created by the use of two or more pieces of photographic film. A filter adopts the same principle – it is laid over a lens (the image) to manipulate the light that reaches our eyes and therefore alter the image that we see.

Image Techniques

Client: This Is A Magazine
Design: Studio KA
Image description:
Overlay of two photographs,
and the inclusion of noise (see
page 7)

Image Filters

The panels below demonstrate the results of various filtering techniques that are available in photo-manipulation applications. Filtering techniques vary from subtle colour adjustments to making dramatic graphic interventions, and provide a designer with many tools for creating design statements.

These images use filters that have coloured overlay screens, which alter the colour of an original photograph.

Left to right: median, noise, dust and scratches, grain, colour halftone and mezzotint filter effects.

Left to right: a solarise of an RGB image and inversion, a CMYK solarise image and inversion and further adjustments.

Left to right: glowing edges, colour adjustment, mosaic, stained glass, fragment and edges filter effects.

Different colour adjustments of original image achieved through the use of filters.

Client: Hulton Archive
Design: Gavin Ambrose
Image description:
Series of images using duotone, median, colour adjustments, painted, overlay and solarisation effects

No dress-code. No inhibitions. No hang-ups. With Hulton Archive you can focus on what really counts.

With hundreds of thousands of images, it's time you embraced

www.hultonarchive.com

Don't just stand on the shoulders of giants, dance on them, boogie with them, romance them.

www.hultonarchive.com

It's your turn now. Take a deep breath. Then take the plunge.

www.hultonarchive.com

There's a whole new universe out there. Explore. Discover. Take the first step. Who knows what you'll find.

Add a splash of colour, a touch of inspiration, and the possibilities for any image are endless

www.hultonarchive.com

Hulton Archive

This invitation was created by Gavin Ambrose for a Hulton Archive exhibition. A series of images have been altered to show the diversity of the photographic archive. Clockwise from top left: a duotone of red and black, median, colour adjustments, a portrait of Frida Kahlo that has been made to look painted, a flag pattern overlay on moon landing and a solarisation of Albert Einstein.

Image Filters

Reveals

Some designs show you everything up front. Others reveal content gradually through the way that they have been physically structured, as the example opposite shows. Reveals may introduce information piecemeal, literally revealing the content or message piece by piece, or they may initially obscure information before it is subsequently revealed to the viewer or user. They are often used to create an interesting visual effect and/or to help structure the information a publication contains. In this context, image placement needs to be considered within the wider context of the format of the publication and any implications of the print finishing required must also be taken into account.

Die cut

A die cut is a process that uses a steel die to cut away a part of the substrate. It is mainly used for decorative purposes; often to enhance the visual performance of a design through the creation of interesting shapes or apertures, and so allows a reader to partially see inside a publication.

Client: Skeleton Key
Design: Sagmeister Inc.
Image description:
Balloon theme revealed
through puncturing die cuts

Skeleton Key

For the 'Fantastic Spikes Through Balloon' album by Skeleton Key, New York agency Sagmeister Inc. produced a design that incorporated photographs of balloon-like objects, such as a sausage and a blowfish, and perforated the substrate with a pattern of die-cut holes. The consistent visual theme is only revealed by looking past the pattern of die-cut holes that puncture all of the 'balloon' shapes.

Incidentally, the lyrics are printed with reversed type because the band did not want people to be able to read them whilst listening to their music.

Image Reveals

Shack Chic:
Art and Innovation in South
African Townships
Craig Fraser
Poems by Sandile Dikeni

Client: Westzone Publishing
Design: Rose Design
Image description:
Details revealed after removal
of a scratch panel

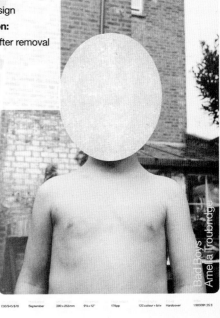

Title
The triumph of artistic tenacity over
adversity is brought to life in Craig Fraser's
vibrant images, which capture the
innovation and talent of South Africa's
shack dwellers. Having focused on some
of the most luxurious homes in the world,
Fraser has found true inspiration in some
of the poorest. Using only available light, he
left the interiors unstyled to better capture
their unique beauty and eclecticism.
This book celebrates the tenacious
decorating spirit that renews and colours
South Africa's urban landscape under
some of the harshest conditions.

Author
Craig Fraser has travelled extensively
shooting the interiors of homes and
commercial installations. He has worked
with Condé Nast, Elle, Carlton Books,
and Quadrille Publishers. His most recent
book, Stylish Living in South Africa, is
published by Struik.

Sandile Dikeni, a poet and columnist,
is the author of two poetry collections,
Guava Juice and Telegraph to the Sky.
His work has been translated into French,
Hebrew and Italian.

£30/$45/$70	September	300 x 255mm	9¾ x 12"	176pp	120 colour + b/w	Hardcover	1903381 253

Shack Chic:
Art and Innovation in South
African Townships
Craig Fraser
Poems by Sandile Dikeni

Title
The triumph of artistic tenacity over
adversity is brought to life in Craig Fraser's
vibrant images, which capture the
innovation and talent of South Africa's
shack dwellers. Having focused on some
of the most luxurious homes in the world,
Fraser has found true inspiration in some
of the poorest. Using only available light, he
left the interiors unstyled to better capture
their unique beauty and eclecticism.
This book celebrates the tenacious
decorating spirit that renews and colours
South Africa's urban landscape under
some of the harshest conditions.

Author
Craig Fraser has travelled extensively
shooting the interiors of homes and
commercial installations. He has worked
with Condé Nast, Elle, Carlton Books,
and Quadrille Publishers. His most recent
book, Stylish Living in South Africa, is
published by Struik.

Sandile Dikeni, a poet and columnist,
is the author of two poetry collections,
Guava Juice and Telegraph to the Sky,
His work has been translated into French,
Hebrew and Italian.

£30/$45/$70	September	300 x 255mm	9¾ x 12"	176pp	120 colour + b/w	Hardcover	1903381 253

Westzone Publishing

This is a small-format brochure produced by Rose Design for Westzone Publishing. Key details in the photographs are revealed only once a scratch-off panel has been removed, such as the face on the boy (shown on the facing page) and the facsimile of a skirt (shown on this page). The act of scratching off the panels makes some surprising revelations!

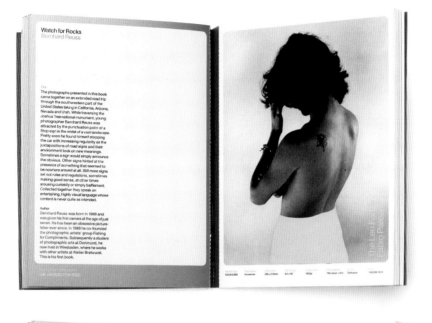

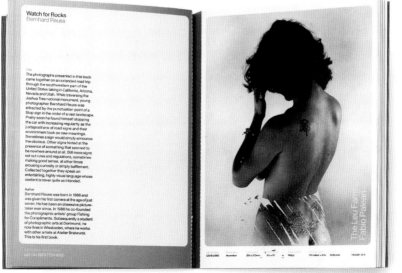

Client: Ron Mercer
Design: Roundel
Image description:
Scratch panels to reveal title
and artist's contact details.

scrape

ron mercer
scraper board illustrator
01453 833755
www.ronmercer.co.uk
scrap

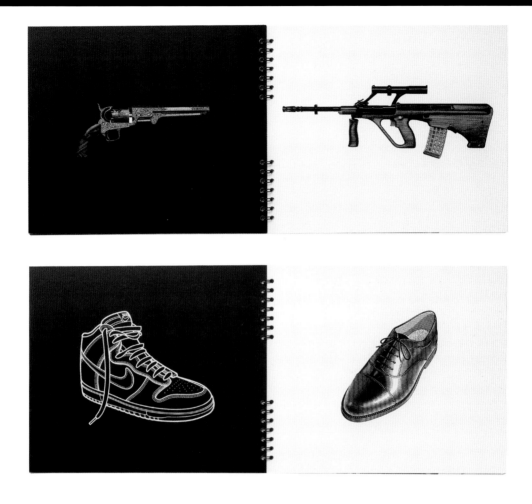

Ron Mercer

Ron Mercer is an illustrator who specialises in the use of scraper boards, Roundel design studio therefore chose to make this trademark a key aspect of their cover design for a catalogue of his work. The name of the artist was concealed underneath a scratch-off panel, which invited people to use Mercer's favoured technique to reveal the information it contained. The publication juxtaposes contrasting images that complement one another and also demonstrate the diversity of Mercer's works and drawing styles.

A scraper board (or Sgraffito)

Sgraffito (from the Italian meaning 'to scratch') describes a technique that allows a top panel of colour to be scratched off, and in doing so reveals a second colour underneath. A scraper board is a substrate that has a removable black top surface over a white subsurface.

Image Reveals

Colouring images

Images are coloured for a number of reasons: to make simple, yet arresting designs, to subtly add different dimensions to a piece, or to create something quite extraordinary.

Images can be coloured in a wide variety of ways and styles ranging from the simple filling-in of forms with graduated colour to altering the colour channels of a photograph. The ways in which an image can be coloured is so broad, and the range so wide that this section will only touch on some of the possibilities.

An image produced and modified as RGB behaves differently to an image produced as CMYK due to the different colour channels used. As most filtering techniques rely on changing light values the differences can be very pronounced, as the images below demonstrate. Each of the three columns uses a different filter (left to right: equalise, invert and channel mixing), however the top row contains RGB images and the bottom row contains the CMYK images, there is clearly a marked difference between the two rows.

Image Techniques

Client: Stereohype
Design: Fl@33
Image description:
Multi-layered line art with
colour fills

Stereohype
This image is part of an identity created by Fl@33 design studio for Stereohype, a London-based online graphic art and fashion boutique. The image is a mix of line-art illustration that is overlaid on a gradient colour, which has been used to fill another part of the design. The use of colour helps provide contrast to the line-art illustration and separate the various layers in the image.

Image Colouring images

The panels below show some of the many ways that a digital image can be coloured. Many of these methods are based on traditional photographic image manipulation techniques, such as altering contrast or adding tints. Technology has enabled the designer to push this further by providing a range of tools on a desktop computer.

Above: manipulating the colour palette, either working in RGB or CMYK to alter the effect.

Above: adding colour tint overlays to the image.

Above: adding and subtracting selective colours.

Above: applying colours can be subtle or more graphic in their output.

Above: using the above techniques to the point of abstraction.

Client: This Is A Magazine
Design: Studio KA
Image description:
A greyscale image with a
graduated tint

This Is A Magazine

This is an illustration by Studio KA for *This Is A Magazine*. It features a greyscale image that has been coloured in a tint, which graduates top to bottom from red to yellow. The result is far more interesting than a simple black and white image and the viewer's attention is naturally drawn to the darker colour – the head of the man.

Greyscale

Greyscale refers to the brightness of a pixel and is expressed as a value representing its lightness from black to white. The term is applied to images that contain a range of shades (of grey), and a range in their depth from black to white.

Image Colouring images

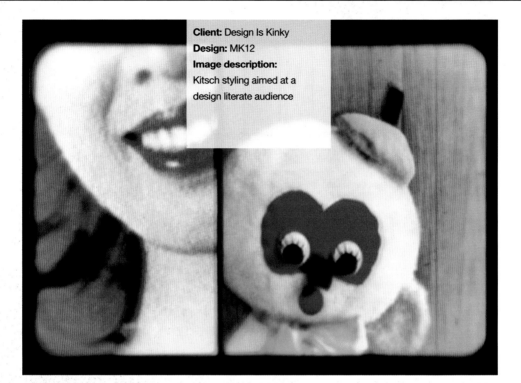

Client: Design Is Kinky
Design: MK12
Image description:
Kitsch styling aimed at a
design literate audience

What Images Mean

Images can have various cognitive and denotive meanings that usually stem from an aspect of a given culture. Designers will often purposefully incorporate symbolic content within a design so that it communicates in a way that is not always obvious. Images generally have a very short time in which to pass a message to the viewer and so various devices are used to communicate meaning quickly and effectively. Images are carefully chosen and presented so that they will convey a specific meaning to a specific group of people. This may be realised through use of symbolism, metaphors, similes or typograms as well as a number of other methods.

For an image to transmit its intended message, a designer must carefully consider the application of some, or all, of the methods covered in this section – as there is always the possibility of unwanted misinterpretation. Subconsciously we all attach meanings to the images that are presented to us. This section aims to analyse some of those meanings.

Design Is Kinky (left)

These are images created by MK12 design studio for *Design Is Kinky*, a magazine and website devoted to design, art and film. An image in isolation or without context is meaningless. The images shown here feature children's toys and a woman dressed in a 1950s style of clothing, so what is the message? Is this about a child's television programme or is this something that has been styled to look this way? The magazine and website are intended for a design literate audience and so the kitsch colouration of the images, coupled with their TV screen framing, create an identifiable value set. In the right context, these images may be considered 'high design', but the context is key here as this interpretation may be too obscure for a non design-literate audience, which may find them childish or outdated.

Semiotics and common terms

Many terms used for describing images derive from linguistic studies, which essentially means that a certain amount of interpretation is required when applying them to the visual form. This section will outline the language and terminology used in the interpretation of images.

Semiotics (the study of signs) and linguistics (the study of language) both offer explanations of how we interpret images. Semiotics has three categories: the sign, the system and the context. The signs below are different shapes. When seen alongside other signs, as they are here, the shapes denote specific meanings: a triangle is a warning of danger, a rectangle imparts information and a circle denotes an order.

1

2

3

These symbols can be broken down into different categories. **Icons** (1) visually represent the item they describe, in this case elderly people. **Index symbols** (2) have a link between the object and the sign, in this example smoke relates to fire. **Symbols** (3) have no inherent relationship with what they are used to describe.

Sign
A word is a signifier and the object that the word represents is what is signified. When these two elements are merged together the result is a sign.

Signified   **Signifier**

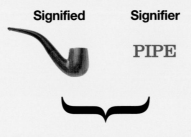

PIPE

Sign

Semiotics

Semiotics is the study of signs and the theoretical principles that underpin how people extract meaning from words, sounds or pictures. Many works of art, plays and novels include symbolic references or signs that communicate additional information.

For example, a statue of a man on a horse seems quite straightforward, but if the horse has only two hooves on the ground and is rearing up, we know that this denotes the rider was killed in battle; if one hoof is off the ground, we know that he died in office, and that if all four hooves are planted on the ground we know that he died after leaving office.

Linguistics

The study of language relies on a shared understanding of signs. Language is formed of phonemes; the word 'car' for example, is made of the phonemes 'c', 'a', and 'r'. When seen in sequence these phonemes spell the word 'car', a sign we know to mean a vehicle that we drive. In this case the shared understanding is of the signs of the alphabet.

Car ⟶

However, these relationships are arbitrary as there is no relationship between the letters 'c', 'a' and 'r', and an image of a car. In Spanish the word for car is 'coche', in French 'auto' and German 'wagen', but all these languages reconcile that specific word to the image of a car. Image interpretation relies on shared understanding. Without a shared agreement about the meaning of the signs, the sign is meaningless.

It must also be remembered that what you see above is not a car but a picture of a car. While there may be shared general understanding of what certain images mean, an image can also contain information that it was not intended to and so the viewer may not interpret it as the designer wanted them to. An image therefore can contain both denotive and cognitive information (see pages 70–71).

Image Semiotics and common terms

Cognitive and denotive meaning

An image communicates in many different ways and on many different levels. The subject, the way in which it has been viewed, the context in which it is presented and the objects that may surround it will all play a part in how the meaning of the image is extracted and interpreted. Images can be interpreted through their cognitive and denotive meanings.

The way in which we interpret an image can be altered dramatically by making changes to the way in which it is presented, as the examples opposite show. Some of our interpretations may be influenced by our previous experience of similar images or contexts of image placement. For example, a coarse reproduction of a halftone image may be interpreted as a newsworthy image.

Denotation
A denotive interpretation means to signify something by a visible sign. For example, 'car' is a denotive that we have associated with a four-wheeled vehicle. Likewise, a picture of a car may denote 'transport'.

Connotation
Many images have cognotive meanings far beyond their denotive interpretations. Cognition refers to things that we have perceived, learned and reasoned. A picture of a house denotes a home – the place where you live; but home has other connotations such as family, security and love.

This is an unaltered image of a woman. It is cropped so that she looks like she is leaning forward and we cannot tell if she is sitting or standing.

A different crop that reveals more of the image, and we can see what she is wearing and that she is sitting down.

Cropping-in on her face suggests a very different take and we may start to focus on what she might be thinking.

When recoloured with a sepia tint the image is given an archival quality that makes it seem as if it is taken from an earlier time.

Reducing the saturation of the tones makes the image look faded and worn, implying that the image may have been displayed in a frame or kept in a wallet.

Converting the image to black and white also ages the photograph and reduces the information that may be provided by the incorporation of colour.

Converting the image to a monotone bitmap dehumanises it and removes the woman from her surrounding environment.

Inverting the colours to create a negative image may suggest a flashback to a past event or even the scene of a crime.

Converting the image to a halftone may make us think it has been clipped from a newspaper.

Image Cognitive and denotive meaning

Typogram

A typogram refers to the deliberate use of typography to express an idea visually, but by incorporating something more than just the letters that constitute the word.

For example, the word 'half' cut in half and displayed with only half visible letters would be a typogram. Another example might be the word 'small' set in 6pt type next to the word 'large' set in 72pt type. While not a common graphic device, a typogram is used to give a rudimentary visual reinforcement to the meaning of the word used to form it. Logotypes – logos formed from type – frequently use typograms as a design element that becomes a key part of the identity.

half

small

large

Symbol™ (right)

This poster was designed by Angus Hyland of Pentagram to promote an exhibition of Pentagram-designed logos at London College of Printing in 2001. This minimalist design focuses on the meaning and function of the word 'symbol', which is displayed as a typogram to refer to the culture of corporate logo design. Using a bold white typeface against a black background, the word 'Symbol' becomes a logo. The transformation from a word into a logo is completed by the application of the registered trademark (™) symbol that also highlights the content of the exhibition.

Client:

London College of Printing

Design: Pentagram

(Angus Hyland)

Image description:

Typogram logo

19.03.2001 - 06.04.2001

School of Marketing & Management
present an exhibition of trademarks
by Pentagram Design

Eckersley Gallery
London College of Printing
Elephant & Castle London SE1 6SB

Symbol™

Synecdoche, metaphor and metonym

'Synecdoche', 'metaphor' and 'metonym' are terms that are used to describe different linguistic devices in which one thing is used figuratively to suggest something else. Each of these terms are closely related and therefore often confused. The same devices also work on a visual level – creating imagery with connotations, symbols and signs. Whether the imagery has meaning above and beyond the literal subject or is simply used for visual impact, it is important to recognise the subtle distinctions between each of the three devices.

The definitions of synecdoche, metaphor and metonym can appear complex, so this spread takes a simple example of the associations that one might make with New York City to highlight the differences between each. In reality, these visual devices are often more subtle and refined, as the examples on the following spread demonstrates.

Visual synecdoche

This term is applied when a part is used to represent the whole, or vice versa. Quite simply, the main subject is substituted for something that is inherently connected to it. This substitution works as long as what the synecdoche represents can be universally recognised and understood, rather than taken at face value for its literal meaning. The ability to refer to a group, or class, of objects through a visual device enables a designer to convey an idea in a clean and unfettered manner. In this example the Statue of Liberty (left), is a landmark in New York, but it has become so synonymous with the city that it can be used to represent New York.

Visual metaphor

A visual metaphor is used to transfer meaning from one image to another. Although the images may have no close relationship, a metaphor conveys an impression about something relatively unfamiliar by drawing a comparison between it and something familiar. In this example the apple (left), is used as a visual metaphor for New York, which is often called The Big Apple. The term was adopted following an advertising campaign that attempted to increase tourism in the 1970s. At that time the city had a poor reputation and it was hoped that the use of an apple as a visual metaphor would create a bright and fresh image of New York.

Visual metonym

A visual metonym is a symbolic image that is used to make reference to something with a more literal meaning. For example, a cross might be used to signify the church. By way of association the viewer makes a connection between the image and the intended subject. Unlike a visual synecdoche, the two images bear a close relationship, but are not intrinisically linked. And unlike visual metaphors, metonyms do not transfer the characteristics of one image to another. In this example, the yellow taxi cab (right), is typically associated with New York, although it is not physically part of the city.

Image Synecdoche, metaphor and metonym

Client: Virgin Records
Design: Form Design
Image description:
Everyday items vibrantly
photographed and used as
visual metonyms

Anomie & Bonhomie (above)

This artwork was produced by Form Design for the Scritti Politti album 'Anomie &
Bonhomie'. It features a series of images of everyday objects that are elevated to
something more important by the use of vibrant photography against a white
backdrop. Some of the images function as metonyms: the crown cap (main picture)
represents a party or other social gathering, and the guitar plectrum and the record
stylus are metonyms of music.

Royal Academy of Music (right)

This literature for the Royal Academy of Music was created by Intro design studio.
It features images that have nothing to do with music, but convey a sense of natural
passion, calm and serenity – qualities that many people will associate with music. The
image is a metaphor because it is used to arouse a set of values and emotions that
the viewer will transfer to the content of the communication. Thus, somebody looking
through the literature may think that the musical events will be serene and soothing.

ROYAL ACADEMY OF MUSIC

**Royal
Academy
of
Music**

Diary
of
Events
**Summer
2004**

Client:
Royal Academy of Music
Design: Intro
Image description:
Visual metaphor used to
describe music

Image Synecdoche, metaphor and metonym

Simile

A simile is a figure of speech that involves the comparison of one thing with another thing of a different kind, such as 'as pure as the driven snow'. Images are commonly used as similes to create a link between a characteristic and an organisation or product. For example, using images of plants might suggest that a product contains natural ingredients; and this in turn may enforce the commonly used simile 'as fresh as a daisy'.

Visual simile

Visual similes are common and work because of the implicit trust and perceived truth that they suggest. For example, if a food product was full of processed ingredients, to use a natural simile to promote it would be a deception. Once the deception was revealed (by tasting the product), it would produce very negative feelings in the consumer and they would be unlikely to trust, or buy, the product again. Visual similes therefore only work if they seem reasonable and are based on an element of truth.

Kenzo (right)

This packaging was created for a line of Kenzo health and beauty products by Research Studios. The leaf design is used as a visual simile to inform potential buyers that the range of products contain natural ingredients. The leaf was photographed from four angles, with one image appearing on each side of the box, so that turning the box is like turning a leaf. This reinforces the simile that the product is as natural and organic as the leaf.

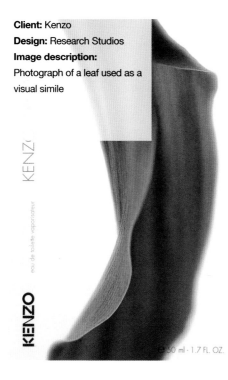

Client: Kenzo
Design: Research Studios
Image description:
Photograph of a leaf used as a
visual simile

Image Simile

Analogy

An analogy is a comparison between one thing and another, made for the purpose of explanation or clarification. For example, a task that is seemingly impossible is analogous to the tasks of Hercules or the fate of Sisyphus who was destined to perpetually roll a rock to the top of a hill only to have it roll back down again. The success of an implicit analogy in a design will be dependent upon the ability of the target audience to see exactly what the analogy is. An image of a man pushing a rock may mean little to some people, whilst others may clearly grasp its intended meaning.

Visual analogy

A visual analogy provides a similarity in visual form between otherwise dissimilar things. As with the chicken (right), an image of something is used to explain or suggest a totally different idea or concept. Visual analogies are usually based on the verbal analogies that populate language because they can be easily interpreted by the viewer. If the analogy is too complex it will be ineffective. That said, complex visual analogies can be used to separate a target audience from other people, which may be a useful design tool.

Client: AIGA

Design: Sagmeister Inc.

Image description:

Simple visual analogy

American Institute of Graphic Arts Conference

Images can convey analogical messages with a power and immediacy that text cannot, as this poster for the national conference of the American Institute of Graphic Arts demonstrates. Stefan Sagmeister's poster depicts a headless chicken, which is used as an analogy for someone that expends a lot of energy running around and doing things, yet makes little progress in any beneficial direction. Here, it has also been used as a metaphor for the graphic arts profession with the suggestion that attending the conference will provide direction and enable the delegate to stop running around like the chicken in the poster.

The illustration was by Peggy Chuang, Kazumi Matsumoto and Raphael Rüdisser with photography by Bela Borsodi and Paint Box work by Dalton Portella.

Image Analogy

Paradigm

A paradigm can be defined as a set of assumptions, common values or practices that constitute a way of viewing reality for the community that shares them. By using images that relate to a particular paradigm a designer can instil a certain set of values and assumptions in a design, which a viewer will readily recognise and accept, if the link is not too far fetched.

Visual paradigm

Paradigms provide a designer with a ready means to communicate a set of values to a target audience by shaping a design with suitable reference keys. For example, many companies try to boost sales by claiming to produce environmentally friendly products. These products are inevitably in green containers, carry images of the rainforest, the sea or wild animals and so on, and as such they trade on poster images of things that environmentalists are trying to preserve.

Barfly (right)

This poster for music venue company Barfly was created by Form Design and uses sticky notes with the names of pop bands handwritten on them. The 'Passport: Back To The Bars' project was a series of concerts held at Barfly venues to raise money and awareness for a number of charities including War Child and Shelter. The design is based on the paradigm that in the modern corporate world, where time is scarce, people write themselves notes to remember important things. In the design, the 'reminders' serve to inform readers of the bands participating and prompt them to participate in an event that is in aid of a charitable cause.

Image What Images Mean

Design: Form² (www.form.uk.com)

Client: Barfly
Design: Form Design
Image description:
Paradigm using sticky notes

Image Paradigm

Client: Dancehouse
Design: 3 Deep Design
Image description:
Black lines used as a visual
metaphor for dance and
dancers

Using Images

The power of a full-page image can speak for itself through its scale and sheer presence. More often than not, however, page space is restricted and an image is only one of several elements that need to be included in a piece. A designer needs to be equipped with different approaches to handling images in order to optimise the graphic content in a design. These techniques include the use of visual continuity, juxtaposition, vista and patterns to enhance the impact and effect that an image has.

An image can be used as a literal example – depicting the object itself under consideration – or it can refer to an emotion, a particular state of mind or it can incorporate some other form of expression according to how it is handled. While images can be used in different ways, making impressive use of them is not an end in itself because the overriding concern of a designer is to produce a harmonious design that communicates effectively to the target audience. As such, it may be necessary to downplay and obscure an image in order to fulfill the purpose of the design.

This section will feature some of the many different ways that images can be used creatively.

Dancehouse (left)
This identity, created by 3 Deep Design for Dancehouse, uses a series of black lines that are displayed at different angles to construct a visual metaphor, which suggests dance and movement. The prominence of the lines and their imprecise, but related, positioning further suggests the arms or legs of dancers.

Continuity

Continuity implies that there is an uninterrupted connection between a given set of items, or that they form part of a coherent whole. Visual continuity means that image elements are somehow grouped together and presented to show that there is a connection between them, or that they are all representative of the same value. Visual continuity can be formed in many ways in a design, these may include the use of duotones to provide visual and colour harmony to different images, converting all images to line art, or using cut-outs.

By applying the same treatment to graphic elements, even quite unrelated images can find common ground. The solution may be as simple as always using picture boxes with rounded corners, applying similar colour palettes or employing consistent cropping techniques.

360° (right)

This is a brochure created by Still Waters Run Deep for the manufacturing arm of Warner Music. A visual representation of a compact disc appears within the '0' on the brochure's cover. This '0' forms part of the '360°' displayed on the front cover – a sparse text reference to the number of degrees in a circle. The circular theme is continued elsewhere in the brochure as it incorporates images of a coconut, the wheel of a car and a balloon; each of which serves as a divider page for sections that talk about distribution and manufacture. The simple and continuous motif is presented as a strong visual element and enhances the brochure, and the motif is reinforced with a spot varnish of a compact disc overlaying each image.

Client: Warner Music
Manufacturing
Design: Still Waters Run Deep
Image description:
Circle theme used throughout,
particularly for engaging
breaker page photography

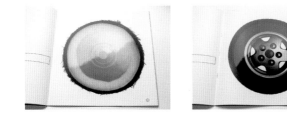

Image Continuity

Juxtaposition

Juxtaposition is the placement of contrasting images side by side. The word is formed from the Latin word 'juxta', which means near, and 'position'.

With regards to image placement, juxtaposition may be used to present two or more visual ideas so as to impart a relationship between them. This relationship may be based on the similarity of their shapes, or an emphasis of the differences between them. This technique extends to the juxtaposition of styles – as shown in the example opposite – where differences or similarities between styles form part of a message. Juxtaposition is frequently used as a device in tandem with other meaningful concepts such as metaphors and similes.

Juxtaposition can be a very strong visual device that allows images to speak without the need for text.
The successful use of juxtaposition in a design depends upon a viewer recognising or interpreting the pairings as intended by the designer. For this reason, juxtapositions frequently employ simple and familiar constructs such as fire and ice (above).

Diesel Range 55DSL (right)
KesselsKramer design studio used architectural models to create fictitious environments under headings such as 'gigs' and 'adult entertainment' to promote the 55DSL range from fashion label Diesel. The images of the environments contain a high level of detailing and are presented in notated comic-strip sequences that juxtapose presentational innocence with the horror of the subject matter.

Client: Diesel Range 55DSL

Design: KesselsKramer

Image description:
Comic-strip images that use architectural models, juxtaposing images of innocence and horror

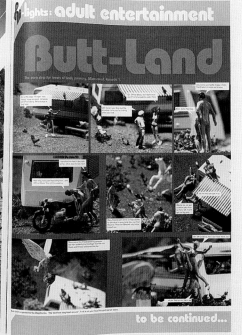

Client: This Is A Magazine
Design: Studio KA
Image description:
Juxtaposed photographic
images and illustrations

This Is A Magazine: Chaos Happens

Designed by Studio KA, this is a compendium of original artwork by more than 60 artists. The book is layered with multi-sized pages and changing formats. It employs a range of printing, binding and folding techniques and a variety of paper stocks as a means of juxtaposing work of different styles. Undersized tip-ins enable the viewer to see the work of two artists simultaneously, and transparent wax paper allows consecutive images to be juxtaposed.

Image Juxtaposition

Vista

Vista, or panoramic, images provide an extended view of the subject matter, which gives the eye more space to explore and move within it. Consequently, they tend to be much longer in the horizontal plane than in the vertical. They may portray natural views or more surreal scenes – as can be seen on this spread.

Once in a Lifetime

This panoramic design by Matthias Ernstberger and Stefan Sagmeister is for the 'Once in a Lifetime' CD box set by Talking Heads. The vista features paintings by contemporary Russian painters Vladimir Dubossarsky and Alexander Vinogradov. The extreme 425 x 135mm format of the packaging provides so much space for a visual narrative to pan across the surface that is almost filmic.

Client: Rhino
Design: Sagmeister Inc.
Image description:
Long format coupled with
panoramic images

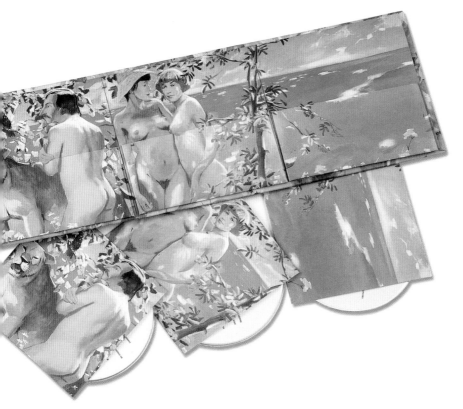

Pattern

In this context, a pattern can be defined as any design that is used as a background. Patterns may be abstract or produced in a metaphoric and representational way. In the example opposite, the pattern used is not only representational of architecture but is also reminiscent of cladding structures on windows and buildings. Examples on the next spread use repetitive geometric patterns instead.

In design terms a pattern can be used as an integral part of a design and so does not always have to be restricted to background use. Patterns can be applied on the surface of a design as a spot varnish, for example, in order to create an interesting visual and tactile effect.

Spot Varnish

A UV spot varnish is a high-gloss varnish that may be applied to select areas of a design in order to enhance their impact, or form part of the overall design. A pattern can be applied to a printed surface using a UV varnish that produces a raised and/or textured surface.

Hurley, Robertson and Associates (right)

This stationery was designed by Gavin Ambrose for architectural practice Hurley, Robertson and Associates. A UV spot varnish pattern has been applied to each of the different items, and this simple design device conveys information about the company and the nature of its work. The pattern, which is reminiscent of structure, order and modernity, was inspired by a particular facia cladding on a building project that the practice worked on.

Image Using Images

Client: Hurley, Robertson and Associates
Design: Gavin Ambrose
Image description: UV spot varnish pattern applied to resemble a building facia

Image Pattern

Client: Thonet

Design: 3 Deep Design

Image description:

Furniture pieces used as icons

in order to create a tessellation

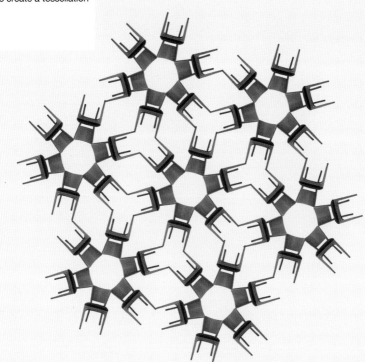

**Erinna
Timberback/
by Thonet**

Marking a new direction for Thonet, this design
has been created to offer an increased level of
comfort. The chair blends bentwood, a moulded
ply back and various upholstery combinations
e.g. fullback, halfback or timberback with
upholstered or timber seat.

Thonet
237 Napier Street
Fitzroy 3065
Victoria Australia
Freecall 1800 800 777
Fax 03 9417 0011

www.thonet.com.au

Thonet

These posters for furniture company Thonet, by 3 Deep Design, feature selected
furniture pieces that are used as icons to form geometric patterns. The resulting
images are at once both contemporary and retrospective, drawing on popular design
styles from the 1960s.

THONET™

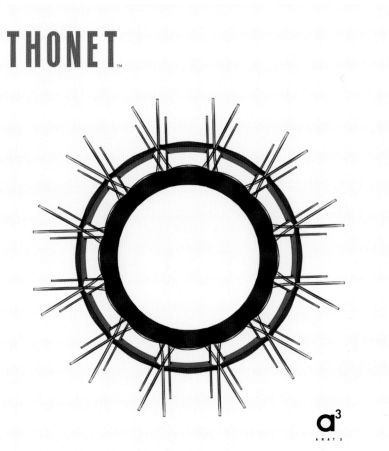

a^3

A N A T 3

Splash Chair
by Jorge Pensi

The Splash Chair, designed by renowned
Spanish designer Jorge Pensi, is framed
in polished anodised aluminium tube.
Seat support in polished injected aluminium.
Seat and back in recycable polypropolene;
colours according to the sample collection.

Thonet
237 Napier Street
Fitzroy 3065
Victoria Australia
Freecall 1800 800 777
Fax 03 9417 0011
www.thonet.com.au

Tessellation

Tessellation is a repeated geometric design that covers a surface without leaving gaps or creating overlaps, and was popularised by Dutch graphic artist Maurits Cornelis Escher. Designs or objects are subsumed into an interlocking pattern and as such the individual elements may not be instantly recognisable.

Image Pattern

Client: Selfridges & Co.
Design: Cartlidge Levene
Image description:
Photographs of kitchenware
taken out of context and used
as graphic pattern

Images in Practice

Images are a powerful means of communicating an idea. Developments in modern printing processes, the rise in popularity of digital photography and the availability and range of image libraries have all contributed towards making photographic images cheaper and more accessible than ever before. However, this has had a direct and detrimental impact on the illustrated image. Contemporary film posters, for example, use photography almost exclusively to promote a movie, but historically illustration was used as the graphic medium of choice for this same purpose.

The ability of a photograph to effectively communicate a message means that they are often used without further embellishment, especially of course in the instance of reportage photography. However, various manipulation methods and presentation techniques exist that can be used to equip a designer with the means to change the appearance of a photographic image, and so achieve the desired effect for any given design. In addition to complex manipulation and presentation techniques, simple methods can be employed by a designer to enhance the impact of an image. For example, incorporating a series of images within a design can provide additional information, as well as a feeling of movement. This chapter will introduce some of the different ways in which photographic images are used by a designer.

Selfridges & Co. (left)
Cartlidge Levene created this fold-out brochure to communicate the architectural inspiration and vision of the new Selfridges store in Birmingham, England – an innovative building designed by Future Systems architects. Within the brochure, powerful imagery of the architecture is combined with photographs of Selfridges' products in an attempt to appeal to potential concessionaires. Pictured here is an array of kitchenware that has been taken out of context and placed against a contrasting background to create an enticing visual element.

Reportage

Reportage is a particular style of photography that is characterised by images which capture those defining and instantaneous moments of real life. Reportage photography captures raw emotions; the joys and horrors of the world around us and helps to define our perception of humanity and the world around us. By their very essence, reportage images can energise a design in ways that photographs taken in a controlled studio environment cannot. The powerful impact of reportage means that it tends to be used without further embellishment by the designer because the images speak for themselves. Non-reportage photographs can also be stylised to simulate a reportage effect.

Client: Hans Brinker Budget Hotel, Amsterdam
Design: KesselsKramer
Image description: Reportage photography focused on the study of a particular bathtub

Hans Brinker Budget Hotel, Amsterdam

This book was produced by KesselsKramer design studio using images by photographer Roy Tzidon. Tzidon spent two months staying in Room 412 of Amsterdam's Hans Brinker Budget Hotel, which is the only room in the hotel that has a bathtub. He invited hotel guests to bathe in the tub in exchange for being photographed. The book that resulted from this project documents the various travellers that passed through the hotel's doors in a series of black and white, and colour images. The book is presented in a towelling drawstring bag, implying a sense of bathtime fun.

Image Reportage

Client: Corbis

Design: Segura Inc.

Image description:

Unadulterated reportage photography

Corbis (above)

These images are taken from a catalogue that was produced by Segura Inc. for photography library, Corbis. The reportage photographs are presented in their original and unaltered form and reproduced as full-page spreads so that the powerful magnitude of the images, and the events they have captured, is uncompromised.

Untitled (right)

This magazine, designed by Bis for Untitled, is printed in a single colour. Photographs that have been captured in a reportage style, are displayed as full-bleed images so as to dominate the spreads and demand attention. The economic production method adds a bleak honesty to, and enhances the gravity of, the content by keeping the presentation simple and not allowing any possible distraction.

Client: Untitled
Design: Bis
Image description:
Featuring qualities of reportage
photography, the monotone
production enhances sincerity

MEXICO WITHOUT CENSORSHIP

"I'M A BELIEVER"

Keith Tyson in conversation with Harry Pye

Portrait of Keith Tyson by Andy Fulton. Courtesy Anthony Reynolds Gallery, London

Image Reportage

Sequence

Some ideas and concepts are difficult to express in a single image; such as motion or instructions that explain how to perform a specific task. Using a sequence of images allows a greater range of ideas to be communicated, although it requires more design space. A sequence of images can depict how action unfolds or provide a series of steps for the viewer to follow.

A collection of images can be presented in ways that change the meaning of a single image. Individual pictures often have little or no relevance until they are juxtaposed with something else. How do you know what is beautiful until you know what is not?

This particular sequence was compiled by Erik Kessels and Julian Germain for their self-published concertina booklet (right), and is subject to their visual sensitivities and personal understanding of its nature. Another person would probably arrange the image sequence differently.

Client: KesselsKramer
Design: KesselsKramer
Image description:
Image sequence deliberately
chosen to stimulate thoughts

Missing Links

This self-published booklet by KesselsKramer design studio features a series of
Polaroid photographs from a collection Erik Kessels formed over a ten-year period.
As the publication has a concertina fold, the images can be viewed in pairs or as a
long sequential strip. With no supporting text to link the images, the reader is asked
to determine the 'missing links' referred to in the title as they pass through the
sequence.

Image Sequence

Client: This Is A Magazine
Design: Studio KA
Image description: Multiple exposure image to convey a feeling of movement

Butterflies and Zebras

This image was produced by Studio KA for *This Is A Magazine*. It was formed from a series of photographs that were overlaid in a specific sequence in order to create a sense of movement, and thus provides a different and more detailed view of the clothes the model is wearing.

Image Images in Practice

Client: 100% Design

Design: Blast

Image description: Images with varying solidity, superimposed to create movement

100% Design

This publication produced by Blast design studio features repeated images of the same piece of furniture. Different photographs of the same object placed in different positions, are superimposed on top of one another with varying levels of solidity to create a sense of movement that visually describes features of the items, such as the ability to reposition the neck of the lamp.

Image Sequence

Blue Source

Design agency Blue Source created a website to showcase its portfolio, which can be clicked through in a similar fashion to the way in which one might flick through the pages of a book. Using the 'unlimited' pages that the internet makes available, the agency included a virtual sketchbook section to showcase a sequence of hundreds of images that may or may not contribute to other ideas. The sparse use of text affords the user the opportunity to interpret the images in multiple ways.

Surrealism

The concept of surrealism finds its origins in a twentieth century avant-garde movement in art and literature. This movement sought to release the creative potential of the unconscious mind, for example, by the irrational juxtaposition of images.

Client: Blue Source

Design: Blue Source

Image description:
Random carrousel imagery in
the surrealist tradition

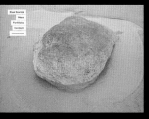

Manipulation

An image can be manipulated to change its appearance, to emphasise or diminish certain aspects within it, or to isolate it completely for use in a design. Image manipulation techniques can achieve some superb results, even with straightforward source material. In our age of vast digital technologies, nearly all the images presented for public consumption are altered, enhanced or 'improved' in some way before they are printed or published.

Client: Diesel
Design: KesselsKramer
Image description:
Manipulation of
model for eternal youth

SAVE
YOURSELF

Contains life-saving advice from Diesel.
With this handy guide to eternal youth, you can be young,
beautiful and sexy forever...
....

Save Yourself

For this brochure for fashion label Diesel, KesselsKramer design studio transformed photographs of the models into images of lifelike dummies. The original photograph of the model is manipulated into a vision of perfect and eternal youth and what results is a reincarnated being that is futuristic and slightly sinister. The message of the campaign is successfully conveyed: a Diesel garment can rejuvenate whoever wears it. As these images demonstrate, the designer's intervention can be subtle or far more obvious, the designer chose the latter option here by replacing the model's hand with a hoof (left).

Image Manipulation

Client: Jum Nakao
Design: Lobo
Image description:
Photography overlaid with
illustration

Jum Nakao

This is a brochure for Brazilian fashion label Jum Nakao, by Lobo design studio.
The photography is manipulated and overlaid with illustrated detail and fine grids
that form a futuristic landscape. A median filter is used on the cut-out photographic
elements to reduce detail. Vector diagrams and illustrations add dynamic colour
and serve as a counterpoint to the simple colouration of the clothes.

Image Manipulation

Client: Coveri
Design: Studio KA
Image description:
Isolated image overlaid on
to a colourful backdrop

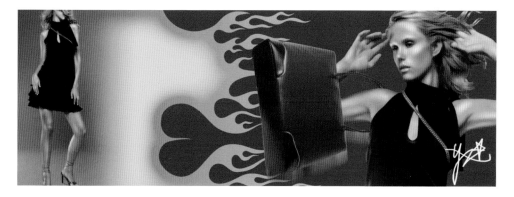

Coveri

These images are taken from a brochure that was created by Studio KA for Italian fashion label Coveri. The featured models have been isolated from their original backgrounds and overlaid against a series of dynamic and colourful backdrops. Skin tones and clothing have been mediated to reduce their tonal balance to a hyper-realistic state. The combination of illustration, photography and image manipulation creates surreal landscapes in which the models become freeze-framed.

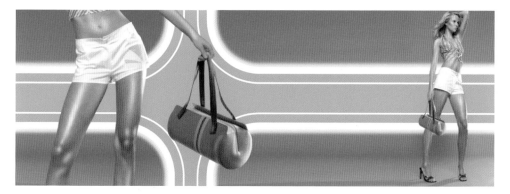

Image Manipulation

Photomontage

Photomontage is a technique whereby two or more images are combined to create a composite. They may be merged seamlessly or with visible joins, but the overall result will be to create an image that benefits from the sum of all parts.

Photomontages can be used to group together different image elements that might not naturally and simultaneously exist, such as people from different historic epochs (shown below), or buildings and landmarks from different countries and so on.

Client: The Design Museum
Design: Studio Myerscough
Image description:
Photomontage created to reflect 1960s styling

THE DESIGN MUSEUM INVITES YOU
TO CELEBRATE THE OPENING OF
ARCHIGRAM ON APRIL FOOL'S DAY
THURSDAY 1 APRIL 2004
FROM 7PM TO 9PM

ARCHIGRAM
3 APRIL – 4 JULY 2004
DESIGN MUSEUM, SHAD THAMES,
LONDON SE1 2YD
WWW.DESIGNMUSEUM.ORG

RSVP ON THE ENCLOSED CARD
ONLY NAMED INVITEES WILL
BE ADMITTED
SUPPORTED BY THE ARTS COUNCIL

Archigram

Studio Myerscough designed this invitation to a retrospective of the work of 1960s avant-garde architects, the Archigram Group. Archigram are renowned for the experimental architecture they produced between 1961 and 1974. The designers chose a visual style from the era during which Archigram – a contraction of 'architecture' and 'telegram' – flourished. One side of the invitation features a photomontage of people and building elements surrounded by a generous white border that is die cut (below). The other side features a triple, multi-coloured outline within which exhibition information is pasted as if it were strips of ticker-tape on a telegram (above).

Image Photomontage

Client: This Is A Magazine

Design: Studio KA

Image description:

Photomontage of photography
and illustration

Compendium 1 (right)

This compendium for *This Is A Magazine was* created by Studio KA. The cover features a monotone collage that is based upon a line drawing of a woman's head. Small photographic elements have then been overlaid on to this to create a surreal image.

Compendium 2 (left)

This cover features a colourful collage that creates a surreal landscape through a combination of photography and illustration. Its execution highlights that the only creative limits are the boundaries of the designer's imagination.

Client: This Is A Magazine
Design: Studio KA
Image description:
Monotone photomontage with photographic elements overlaid on line drawing

Image Photomontage

Collage

Collage is a technique that was popularised by Georges Braque and Pablo Picasso. At the turn of the twentieth century both artists began to produce work that incorporated pieces of printed paper. This rudimentary form of the technique has since been expanded to include other materials. Therefore, a collage can be defined as any material that has been fixed to a surface in order to create an image.

Collage is a creative technique that allows the inclusion of many different objects in a design, although that design may still be based upon one key image that has been deconstructed or composed of different elements – as can be seen in the example opposite.

Malcolm McLaren (right)

This is a limited edition poster for an exhibition about Malcolm McLaren by Why Not Associates. The poster is an eclectic collage of several different elements, including a wide variety of typefaces and images. As such, the design illustrates that the exhibition itself features a collection of personal effects belonging to an individual whose career has turned in many diverse and interesting directions.

Client: Malcolm McLaren
Design: Why Not Associates
Image description: Collage of typography and image

Image Collage

Montage

A montage is a pictorial composition, which is constructed by juxtaposing and/or superimposing a number of pictures or designs to form a new image. This can be seen in the example opposite, where the different elements are united to create a new image form.

It is important to understand that although they are similar techniques, montage and collage can be clearly distinguished. A montage contains separate elements that are brought together to form another independent image or design. A collage is a more random composition of elements that do not, ultimately, create another image.

Cityscape Insects (right)

This design was commissioned by Paris-based advertising agency Les Quatre Lunes for the 2003 annual report of Groupe Galeries Lafayette / BHV. Created by Fl@33 design studio this montage 'Cityscape Insects' was inspired by *trans-form magazine*. In this montage, rolls of fabric and office stationery are brought together to create a single pictorial image of an insect.

Client: Les Quatre Lunes
Design: Fl@33
Image description:
A montage of fabric rolls and
office stationery to create a
surreal creature

Image Montage

Cropping

Cropping is a technique that cuts away extraneous material from the edges of a photograph so that the focus is retained on a specific part of it.

Generally, the rule of thirds is employed when cropping an image so as to ensure optimum results. The frame is divided into nine equal parts by creating a mental grid – as illustrated below. A key feature of the photograph, in this case an eye, is placed at any of the four central points where the lines of the grid bisect.

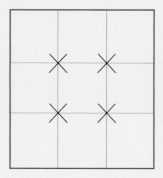  

Experimentation with these four positioning points can produce a variety of dramatic results.

In this example (right), the crop has been used to instil an unexpected tension in the image.

Client: Kenzo

Design: Research Studios

Image description:

Close, unusual image crop coupled with median filter to reduce detail and tone gradation

FLOWERBYKENZO

Flower by Kenzo

This promotional poster for Kenzo's signature scent was created by Research Studios. This image was manipulated using a median filter that reduced its level of detail and tone gradations. The resulting dreamy and almost vague image contrasts with the pinpoint detail of the perfume bottles situated beneath it. This impression is further compounded by use of a close crop that focuses attention on the woman's neck and removes her eyes, usually a key focal point.

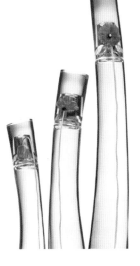

KENZO

Image Cropping

Trompe l'oeil

Trompe l'oeil is an image technique that concerns optical illusions and intentional visual deceptions. Literally meaning 'trick of the eye' it applies to an object, image or design that creates the illusion of reality, or of being something that it is actually not. For example, the cover of the project on the facing page appears to be three-dimensional when it is, in fact, a flat surface.

Trompe l'oeil may be employed within a design to deliberately confuse a viewer, or to provide information only to those that form a specific target audience who will be able to interpret the message.

Hoogstraten Catalogue (above and right)

Faydherbe / De Vringer created this catalogue to display the work of Dutch artist Jeroen Hoogstraten for Centrum Beeldende Kunst Provincie Utrecht. It was designed to reflect the fact that Hoogstraten moves between the disciplines of industrial design and fine art in his work. The catalogue design borrows elements from trade manuals, which results in something fresh and diverse. The trompe l'oeil cover creates a faux 3D effect and mirrors the 'constructed' works that are showcased within the catalogue.

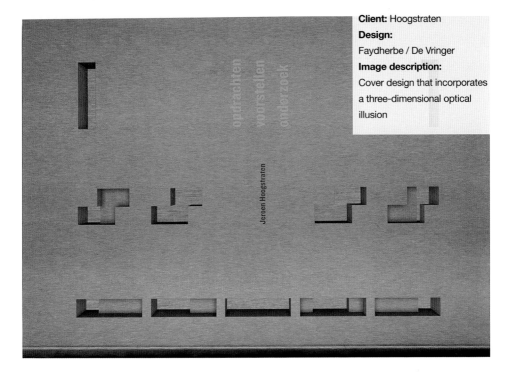

Client: Hoogstraten
Design:
Faydherbe / De Vringer
Image description:
Cover design that incorporates
a three-dimensional optical
illusion

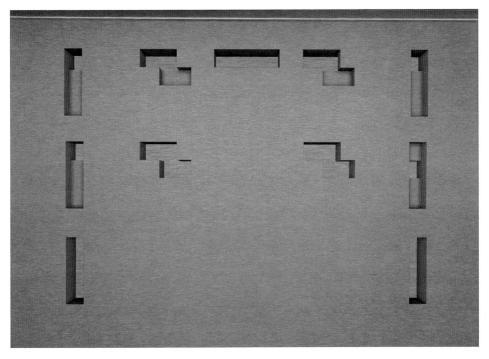

Image Trompe l'oeil

Pointillism

Pointillism is a form of painting that was pioneered and popularised in the nineteenth century by French painter Georges Seurat. Its name derives from the brushwork required to form the tiny dots of primary colours that, when viewed from a distance, merge to produce the secondary colours. Television screens work on a similar principle.

With computer technology, any image can be given a pointillistic treatment. To do so requires that the image is rasterised, or converted into individual pixels of information, so that it can be manipulated by a drawing program as the simple examples in this section demonstrate. This technique can create visually unique and exciting results.

The opposite page features a series of experimental interpretations of the pointillistic technique. The same image has been used to clearly show some of the different effects that can be achieved.

At the bottom of this image of a sunflower a single point has been highlighted. Each point in the image is formed by a circle that has been filled with a lighter colour, which produces a translucent effect.

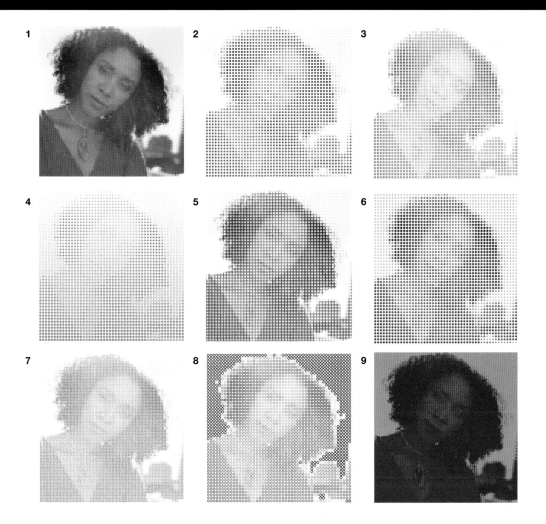

1 This is a full-colour image covered by a pointillist pattern. The square pattern has been lightened so that it stands proud of the background. **2** This image is formed from a straightforward pattern of solid, circular dots. The size of these dots or the spaces between them can be altered to create a denser or lighter image. **3** This image is produced with a pattern of circles that overlays a grid of squares. As with the image of the sunflower on the opposite page, the circles in the centre of the squares have been lightened so that there is sufficient contrast between them without obscuring the image. **4** This image uses an array of circles that have three parts: two concentric circles surrounding an inner one. The largest circles are coloured by a horizontal blend from light to dark. **5** The same treatment as the previous image, but with a far brighter pattern of squares overlaying the full colour image. **6** This image uses three-part circles that have varying levels of colour contrast, which creates a more graphic interpretation. The circles are concentric circles – each circle is smaller than the one it sits in. **7** The dots for this image are a very fine grid of squares, again with a light element surrounded by a dark element. **8** This image is enhanced by a pattern of graphic borders. **9** Here we see the image with heavily-adjusted colours and a magenta bias.

Image Pointillism

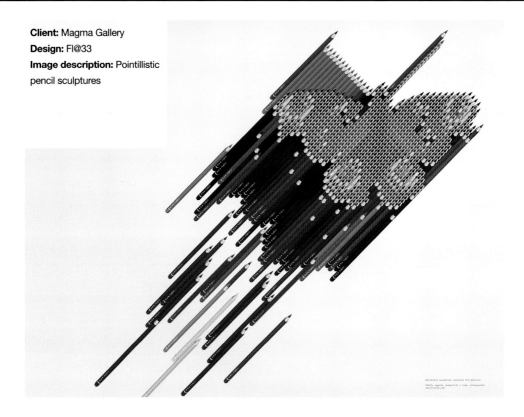

Client: Magma Gallery
Design: Fl@33
Image description: Pointillistic
pencil sculptures

Butterfly Sculpture Contains 818 Pencils (above)

This unique image was produced by Fl@33 design studio as part of a series of pencil sculpture illustrations for the *GB: Graphic Britain* book launch at the Magma Gallery in London. Contrary to what one might expect the points of the actual pencil are used to create a pointillistic effect rather than being used to make marks on the substrate.

V-Series (right)

This work was an in-store promotion for Nike V-Series and was created by Spin design studio. It uses the typographic characters produced by a dot-matrix printer to create a narrative on a continuous sheet of paper. Typographic characters are used as pointillistic dots to form text and images that are used as an engaging presentation of Nike's new product range.

Client: Nike
Design: Spin
Image description:
Typographic characters are
used as pointillistic dots

With or without fonts a series of talks about type
presented by Creative Review and sponsored by Agfa Monotype

New type design

Pentagram 11 Needham Road London W11 2RP Wednesday 19 February 2003 6.30 PM
tickets £10 students £7.50 email aminah.marshall@centaur.co.uk telephone Gavin Lucas 020
in association with Pentagram Design and Gavin Martin Associates

Client: Creative Review and AGFA Monotype

Design: Pentagram (Angus Hyland and Sharon Hwang)

Image description: Pointillistic portrait using ten-dot typeface

Pioneers of modernist typography #1

El Lissitzky was born Lazar Markovich Lisitski on November 23, 1890, in Pochinok, in the Bir province of Smolensk. He pursued architectural studies in Darmstadt, Germany (1909-1914) at received a diploma in engineering and architecture from the Riga Technological University.

In 1919 El Lissitzky was invited by Marc Chagall to join the faculty of the Vitebsk Popular Art School, where he taught graphics and architecture. In the same year he executed his first *Proun* (an acronym in Russian for 'project for the affirmation of the new'), designed the famous Soviet propaganda poster *Beat the Whites with the Red Wedge*, and also formed part of the *Unovis* group. In 1920, he became a member of *Inkhuk* (Institute for Artistic Culture) in Moscow and designed his book *Pro dva kvadrata*. The following year, he taught at Vkhutemas with Vladimir Tatlin and joined the Constructivist group. In 1922 he completed *Of Two Squares*, a children's book.

In 1923, he experimented with a new typographical language for Vladimir Mayakovski's book *Dlya golosa*, and visited Hanover, where his work was shown under the auspices of the Kestner-Gesellschaft. During the same year, he created his *Proun* environment for the Grosse Berliner Kunstausstellung and created his lithographic suites *Proun* and *Victory over the Sun* (the latter illustrating Meyerhold's play of the same name). In 1924, he worked with Kurt Schwitters on the *Nasci* issue of the periodical *Merz*, and with Hans Arp on the book *Die Kunstismen*.

The following year he returned to Moscow to teach at Vkhutemas-Vkhutein, where he remained until 1930. His pivotal role in typographic theory is acknowledged by Jan Tschichold in his seminal text *Die neue Typographie* (1928). El Lissitzky died on December 30, 1941 in Moscow.

Type on screen

Typography by hand

With or Without Feet

These posters were produced by Pentagram for the *With or Without Feet* series of discussions, which were about typography and hosted by design magazine *Creative Review* and AGFA Monotype at the offices of Pentagram design studio.

The promotional posters each feature a portrait of one of three pioneers of modernist typography: Herbert Bayer, Max Bill and El Lissitzky. The portraits are created using a custom made, ten-dot typeface that produces an effect similar to the effects achieved by employing pointillistic techniques – the image only becomes recognisable when viewed at a distance. Pointillism serves to wash out or dilute much of the information that we would expect to see in an image, resulting in sometimes ghostly images as is typified in these portraits.

Image Pointillism

Client: Dangerously Bold

Design: Segura Inc.

Image description:

Mark making used to create an anarchic and 'dangerous' effect

Mark Making

All images communicate via the associations that we attribute to them and what we relate those associations to. This principle extends to basic mark making, and is the reason it is a widely used design technique. Mark making ranges from simple line work, which is often used as metaphoric representation (as can be seen opposite), through to silhouettes, icons, symbols and pictograms. Many of these terms, although familiar, are often misused. For example, the difference between a symbol and an icon is often misunderstood because the terms have become (inaccurately) interchangeable.

Within this section we will explore some of the basic terms used to describe image types, and look at how the marks that these terms describe can be enhanced through creative printing techniques. Even within the constraints of the four-colour printing process there are many ways to embellish an image. Overprinting and creative halftone effects offer a range of adjustments to the way an image can be reproduced. It is necessary for the designer to have a sound understanding of how these effects are created, as they are often only specified to a printer and realised at the proofing stage of a job. Understanding these functions minimises changes, and therefore controls cost and time budgets. It also allows the designer to manage the process rather than allowing the process to control the design.

Dangerously Bold (left)

To produce a pertinent design for Dangerously Bold, Segura Inc. design studio created a stencil that incorporated outlines of potentially lethal objects such as a bomb, a shark, a dagger or a sensei. These are all visual analogies to something that is potentially dangerous. So why not just use pictures of these instead? Creating a design that encapsulated the concept of 'bold' must have been quite a challenge, but a stencil is an effective solution. As you draw around the outline of the object and fill it in, you create a bold impression on the page. The recipient thus gets to have fun mark making with the company's promotional piece.

Silhouette

A silhouette is the representation of an image outline against a contrasting background. Though lacking detail, a silhouette can be used to present a stronger and more definite image of the object. Conversely, a silhouette may also be used to obscure the origins of the object in order to create a sense of mystery.

Using a silhouette allows a designer to take ownership of objects and present them in a consistent manner. In the example opposite the household objects are presented on the invitation in a cool, sophisticated way as gold silhouettes. If they were displayed as full colour images, the job would look more akin to a traditional catalogue.

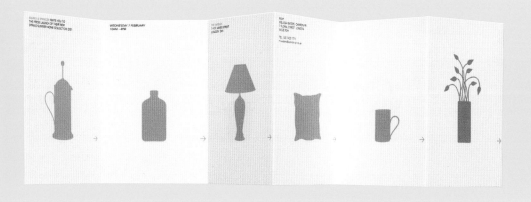

Marks & Spencer Invitation (above & right)

This invitation for an event for food, clothing and household goods retailer Marks & Spencer features standard household objects that hint at the breadth of its product range. The images are printed as a gold silhouette on a concertina foldout, and as such have a solidity, gravity and elegance; qualities that Marks & Spencer would wish their customer to associate with the objects themselves. The gold colour used also corresponds to the colour of the company's logo.

Image Mark Making

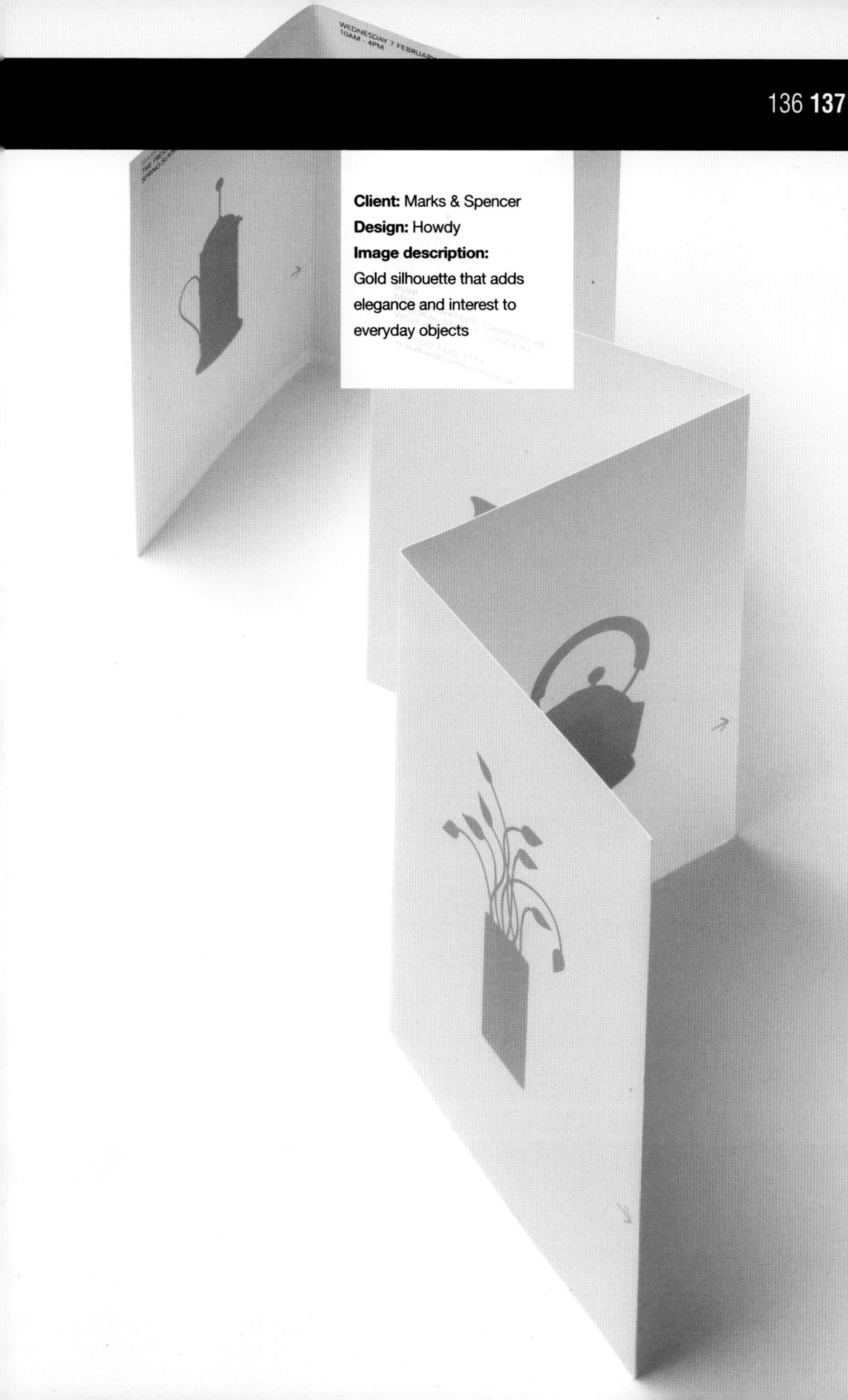

Client: Marks & Spencer
Design: Howdy
Image description:
Gold silhouette that adds
elegance and interest to
everyday objects

Client: The Pavement
Design: Roundel
Image description:
Silhouettes created by
photographing from ground
level

the pavement ...urtain Road London EC2A 3BS T +44 (0)20 7749 4300
F +44 (0)20 7749 4... .com www.the-pavement.com

the pavement Burh·
F +44 (0)20 7749 4·

The Pavement Studios Limited Registered Office 10 Dover Street London W1S 4LQ Registered in England No 3890033 V...

The Pavement

This is an identity and stationery range created by Roundel design studio for London-based DVD production company The Pavement. The website (facing page) was created by State Design. The images of a dog and man are photographed from below, which makes the soles of their feet prominent and also serves as a visual reference to the name of the company, as we view them both from underfoot. The use of a monotone silhouette is simple, playful and has a strong visual impact even though it incorporates little detail. This is further enhanced through displacement of perspective and scale.

Image Mark Making

Client: The Pavement
Design: State Design
Image description:
Implementation of identity
designs on to website

The Pavement is one of Europe's leading award-winning DVD production facilities based in London's Shoreditch/Hoxton area. Renowned for its edge in music and design talent, we work with a wide variety of clients distributing film, music and television programmes as well as artists who simply want to use DVD as a convenient platform to display their work. ▶ ı

a new angle on dvd production

the pavement

The Pavement turns 4

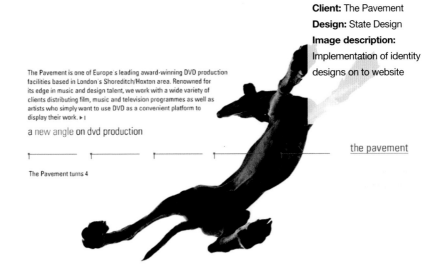

Perspective

Perspective concerns the way that we look at a topic or subject. Exploring unusual perspectives of familiar things in the world around us, as in this example, can provide striking results.

Our producers will help you grasp the intricacies of DVD title development from the simplest of looping videos to interactive hybrid projects. The entire production can be managed, including storyboards, schedules, video shoots and edits, recording studios, third party suppliers (such as subtitle and replication companies), graphics and postproduction.

In our four years producing high-end DVD titles, we have found that the most successful projects arise from clear communication between clients and suppliers and a thorough understanding of DVD's potential and its occasional pitfalls.

the pavement resources - production

resources

the pavement

1 2 3 4 5 6 7 8 9

contact us
watch showreel

The Pavement was established as an independent, forward-thinking DVD production facility in February 2000. Our founders - Andy Evans, Kristen O'Sullivan and Lloyd Shaer - have worked in the DVD industry since it's infancy. They launched Stream - one of the UK's first DVD facilities - for Carlton Communications in 1998, before bringing together an experienced team to form The Pavement. Together, we've worked hard to set the creative and technical standards that have earned us an international reputation.

a brief history of the pavement - 1

history

the pavement

1 2

contact us
watch showreel

BBC Training and Development	EMI	Paramount	Universal Pictures
BBC Worldwide	Entertainment Rights	Reader's Digest	Universal Music
Big Brother Records	Glaxo Smith Kline	Serpentine Gallery	V2 Music Group
Carlton Visual	I-D Magazine	Sony Music	VCI
Channel 4	MGM	The Stationery Office	Warner Home Video
Columbia Records	Momentum Pictures	Strongroom	Warner Vision
Columbia Tristar	onedotzero	Technicolor	Zomba Records
Decca	Opus Arte	Underworld	
Eagle Vision	Orbital		

the pavement client list

clients

the pavement

1 2

contact us
watch showreel

Strongroom - www.strongroom.com

The Pavement's collaborative partner for all audio
and music productions.

the pavement links

links

the pavement

1 2 3 4 5 6

contact us
watch showreel

Image Silhouette

Overprinted Forms of Everyday Objects

This limited edition artists book design by Hector Pottie at Cartlidge Levene features silhouettes of everyday objects such as a fire extinguisher and a cable drum, which are overprinted in red, black and grey on to a stark white background. By overprinting (see page 156), the objects merge together to form morphed, abstract and silhouetted shapes that are accentuated by the absence of typography.

Client: Self-published
Design: Cartlidge Levene
Image description:
Individual silhouettes merged to form abstract patterns and shapes

Overprint

An overprint (or surprint) describes a process in which one ink is printed over another. The technique is used to add texture and multiple layers of information to a design. The order in which the inks are printed will affect the final visual appearance as different printing orders will create different colours, because of this overprints must be considered carefully so that colours reproduce as intended.

Image Silhouette

Icons

An icon is a graphic element that represents an object, person or something else. Icons should not be confused with symbols or pictograms, which have their own specific definitions – as you will see in the pages that follow.

Generally speaking, an icon is a simple reduction of an object such that it is instantly recognisable for what it is, as shown in the three examples below. The simplified presentation of an icon means that the viewer should have little trouble identifying what it represents. In the example opposite, the viewer should recognise that the icons are of spaceships, nothing more nothing less.

Presented with a photograph of a car in a street, the viewer may be distracted by other elements such as the people in it or the buildings and pedestrians in the background. A car icon leaves no doubt that the message concerns, and the central focus of the image is, a car.

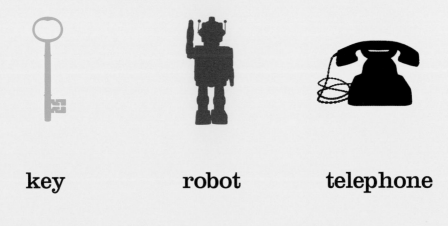

| key | robot | telephone |

T-26

This is a poster created by Segura Inc. design studio to promote type foundry T-26. The poster features icons that can be purchased in one of the font packages produced by T-26. The icons are rendered in a simple retrospective style, which helps to make them function clearly – there are no distracting elements, just the icons.

Image Mark Making

Client: T-26
Design: Segura Inc.
Image description:
Poster formed of font icons

Symbols

Symbols are usually used to communicate the concepts, ideas or objects that they represent, as opposed to describing what they pictorially display. For example, many people would make the connection that the red cross, as used in the example on the opposite page, somehow relates to the English football team because of the context in which it is used.

The ease with which common symbols can be recognised makes them a powerful design tool. A company could use a symbol such as the cross of St George to attract football fans to its product or services. However, potent symbols will be used specifically to reach more people than the immediate target audience.

Potent symbols are read in different ways by different groups. Consequently there is a risk of alienating people that attach negative connotations to symbols. Non-football fans may associate the cross of St George with rowdy football hooligans and as such form a negative view of the company using it.

Image Mark Making

This cross could be a mathematical symbol for addition.

A red cross is ambiguous because it looks out of place against a yellow background.

Against a white background the red cross is more specific, and would be associated with something medical.

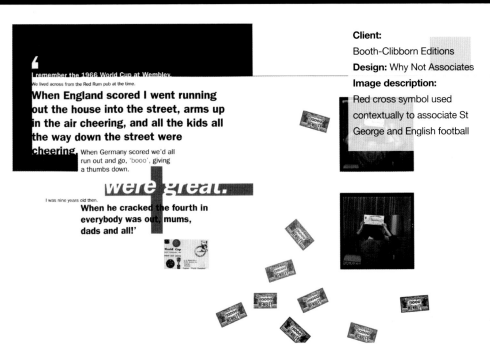

Client:

Booth-Clibborn Editions

Design: Why Not Associates

Image description:

Red cross symbol used contextually to associate St George and English football

'I remember the 1966 World Cup at Wembley. We lived across from the Red Rum pub at the time. **When England scored I went running out the house into the street, arms up in the air cheering, and all the kids all the way down the street were cheering.** When Germany scored we'd all run out and go, 'booo', giving a thumbs down. *were great.* I was nine years old then. **When he cracked the fourth in everybody was out, mums, dads and all!'**

In Soccer Wonderland

This design was created by Why Not Associates for *In Soccer Wonderland*, a book by photographer Julian Germain. The book features photographs and football ephemera. Football incorporates strong visual identities; from the colours of the football strips and club badges, to the leading players who are often recognised as celebrities and as such are used to promote a diverse range of associated products. Football has appropriated some symbols for its own ends such as the cross of St George (a red cross on a white background) that England fans commonly wear on clothing.

Image Symbols

Pictograms

A pictogram is a visual reference or pictorial symbol for a letter, word or phrase. The written form of many languages, for example Chinese, is pictogrammatic because the characters visually represent the word. Pictograms communicate through the associations that we attach to an image or group of images. Their success in a design therefore depends upon how both the target and non-target audience respond to the images; what is acceptable to one demographic may be offensive to another.

It is not always necessary to have an obvious connection between the pictogram and what it is representative of as long as the reader can establish what each pictogram denotes, as the example opposite shows.

Image Mark Making

Client: Pat Metheny Group
Design: Sagmeister Inc.
Image description:
Pictograms used to represent
individual letters

Imaginary Day

This design was created by New York design studio Sagmeister Inc. for the
'Imaginary Day' CD by the Pat Metheny Group. The cover artwork features the name
of the group and title of the album represented in pictograms. Pictures of different
objects have been used to represent the different letters – although the association
between the two is not obvious; for example, a tree represents the letter 'P'. The key
to deciphering the pictograms is the visual rebus, which is printed around the edge
of the CD (facing page).

Rebus
A rebus is an enigmatic representation of a word by pictures (pictograms). A rebus is most commonly seen in a
puzzle, and the aim of the puzzle is to decode the pictograms, which have been used to represent different
syllables and/or words, and construct the hidden message.

Image Pictograms

Photograms

A photogram (or rayograph) is a photograph that is created without a camera. The image is made by placing an object on to light-sensitive material and exposing it to light. The resulting image is a negative silhouette. This technique was pioneered by seminal photographer Man Ray.

A variety of methods have evolved to produce photograms, ranging from the use of filtered light, patterns and motion, to the use of chemicals that modify the light-sensitive material. The results obtained can be easy to recognise or they can be spectacular and peculiar like the photograms on the facing page.

Photograms are not widely used because they do not capture the intricate levels of detail often required in a design. However, their relative scarcity makes their surreal and abstract nature even more striking and unexpected.

Kenzo Ki (right)

These advertisements were created by Research Studios for a range of skincare products by fashion label Kenzo. They feature photograms to represent the key ingredients in each product. The abstract photograms visually represent both the content and nature of each product.

Clockwise from top left: bamboo leaf (energising), ginger flower (euphoric) white lotus (relaxing) and rice (sensual). The images serve a dual purpose as they are arresting and arouse curiosity in the viewer to find out more. The stark whiteness also reflects the natural ingredients used in the skincare range.

Image Mark Making

Client: Kenzo

Design: Research Studios

Image description:
Photograms to convey content
and associated emotions

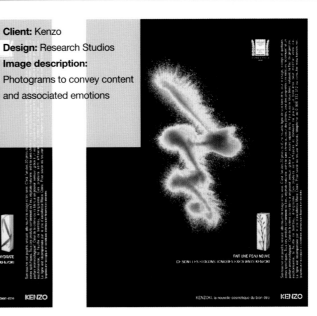

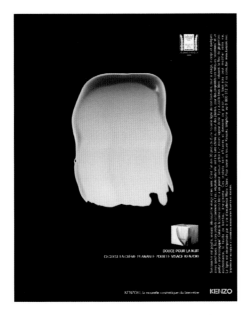

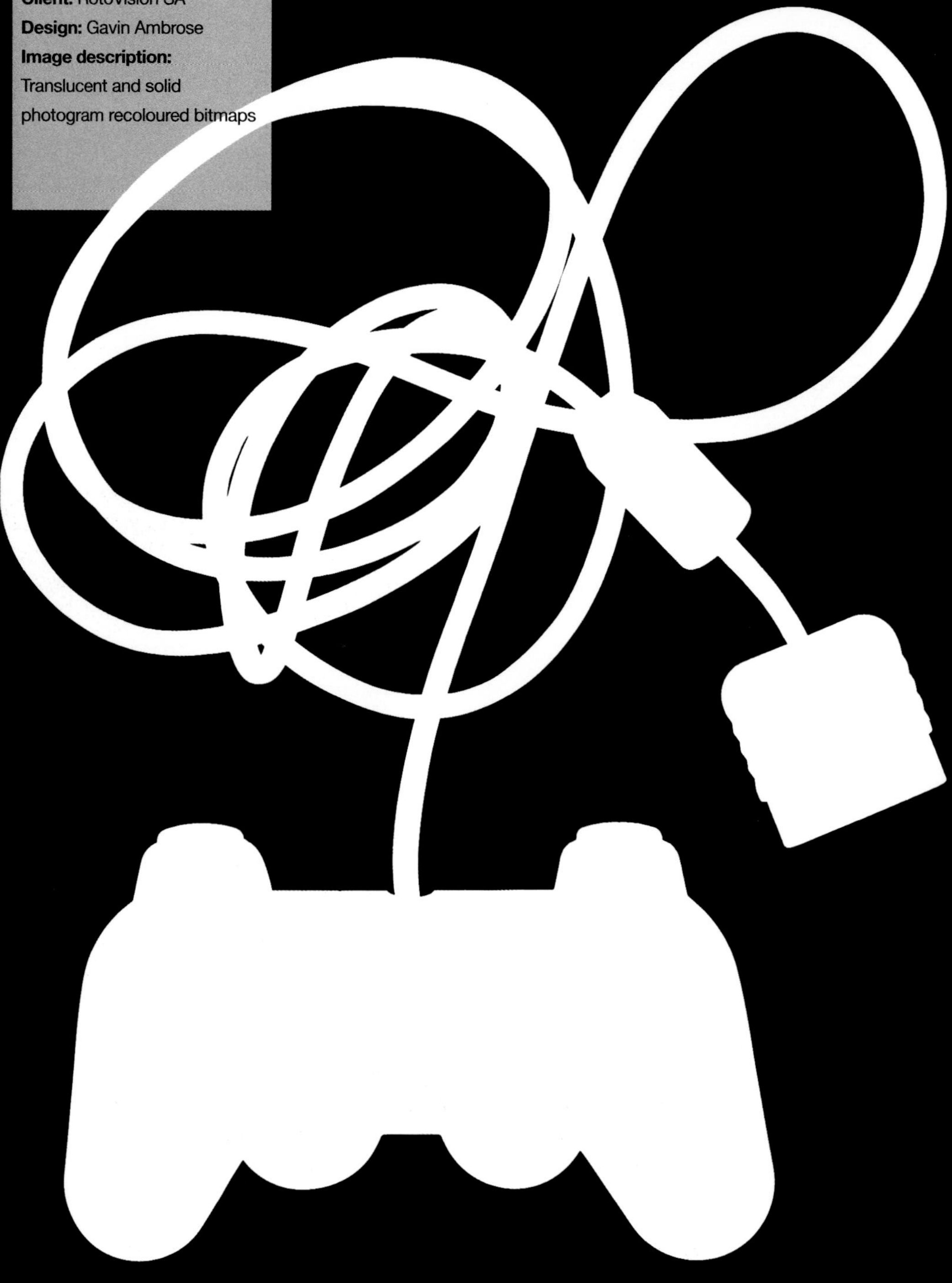

Client: RotoVision SA
Design: Gavin Ambrose
Image description:
Translucent and solid
photogram recoloured bitmaps

Image Mark Making

This End Up

This series of photograms was produced by Xavier Young for use in *This End Up*, a book about packaging design by Gavin Ambrose and Paul Harris. The images were used as a series of related breaker pages. The abstraction of the objects is created by a combination of their translucency and the colour palette with which they are presented. The games controller (opposite), forms a strong silhouette while the more translucent objects (above), appear to be more three-dimensional. The images were created as bitmaps, which enabled them to be coloured independently so that the backgrounds and the images could have been displayed in any colour.

Image Photograms

Halftones

Printers use line screens to convert a continuous tone image, such as a photograph, into a composition of dots – the resulting image is called a halftone. Images that are suitable for the four-colour offset lithography printing process are composed of microscopic dots. Both the pattern and size of the dots can be changed and manipulated to achieve various creative effects.

Halftone effects

The quality of a halftone is controlled through the values of the halftone frequency, screen angle, and function or shape of the dots.

The halftone frequency relates to the lines per inch (LPI), which determines the size of the dot used to reproduce an image and thus its clarity or coarseness. A lower value will produce a more graphic effect while a high value will simulate a photographic effect.

The halftone dots are usually arranged at a particular angle; this is called the screen angle. In a greyscale image the screen angle is normally 45 degrees because this value provides the least distortion to the image.

The function or shape of the dots can be altered from the conventional circle setting, and as you will see, there are many more graphic options available. Generally, the more the dot shape is altered, the more distorted the image becomes. When attempting something more adventurous, this can be an advantage.

Image Mark Making

60 LPI, screen angle of 45 degrees, dot pattern
The magenta lines on each of the images above show the screen angles used to produce them. This image uses a standard 45 degree angle and a low LPI, which means it has coarse dots.

150 LPI, screen angle of 15 degrees, dot pattern
This image has more of a photographic quality because its higher LPI value gives a closer approximation to a continuous tone.

133 LPI, screen angle of 75 degrees, dot pattern
This image also has a more photographic quality with a similar LPI value to the previous image, but note the effect that a different screen angle has.

Dot shape, 60 LPI
This image is formed from the standard circular dot.

Line shape, 60 LPI
This image is formed using a line-shaped dot.

Ellipse shape, 60 LPI
This image is formed using an ellipse-shaped dot.

Image Halftones

Colour halftones
A colour halftone is a halftone image that has been produced using different coloured dots.

This may be done specifically to create an exaggerated impression of the halftone dots used in the four-colour printing process. The result is a cruder picture, which is similar to those seen on bill posters or in daily newspapers. The resulting image seems more immediate, current and raw.

Controlling a colour halftone is fairly simple, as you can alter the radius (dot) size and the angles that each of the four colours print at.

This is the standard and unaltered image.

This image has a small dot radius.

This image has a wider radius, which results in a coarse picture.

Changing the screen angles for the different colours creates a variety of moiré patterns.

Here, the screen angles have been set to similar values.

The dots in this image have a very small radius and altered screen angles.

Image Mark Making

Client: D&AD
Design: Frost Design
Image description:
Colour halftone used to create
a reportage effect

D&AD

The cover image for D&AD's annual *Posedown*, which was created by Frost Design,
features colour halftones of bodybuilders. The colour halftones suggest reportage
photography and provide a rawness to the images; this is combined with slab-serif
type to create a muscular feel to the publication.

Image Colour halftones

Overprinting

An overprint occurs when one element of a design is printed over another. This technique is used to add texture and create multiple layers of information within a design. The overprinting of different inks will create different colours and so it is sometimes necessary to knockout or trap the ink.

Ink trapping refers to the overlapping of areas of coloured text or shapes to account for misregistration on the printing press. The process is required because the halftone dots that make up printed images are all of different sizes and are arranged at different screen angles. The colours are overlapped to prevent the appearance of white gaps.

A knockout refers to the gap left in the bottom ink layer. This gap is left so that any image which overlaps it will appear without colour modification from the bottom layer of ink. The bottom colour is literally 'knocked-out' of the area where the other colour overlaps.

Knockout

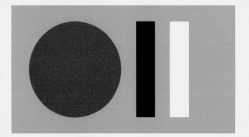

Overprint

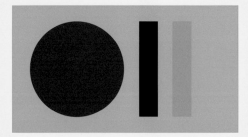

Here, all the shapes knockout of the cyan square and so they remain pure and unadulterated. In simple terms, a hole is created in the cyan for the magenta circle and the yellow and black rectangles to sit in.

In this example all the shapes overprint the cyan square, and so the colours mix.

Image Mark Making

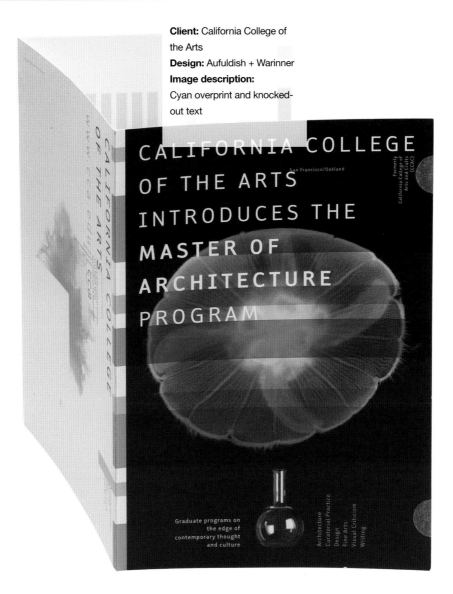

Client: California College of the Arts
Design: Aufuldish + Warinner
Image description: Cyan overprint and knocked-out text

California College of the Arts

This is a brochure for the California College of the Arts, which was created by Aufuldish + Warinner. It features a cyan stripe pattern that is overprinted on to a black halftone and the cover text is knocked out. The colour stripe adds a visual dimension in a cost-effective way (as two-colour printing is cheaper than four-colour printing), but the design means that this simple two-colour job appears to be more substantial than it actually is.

Image Overprinting

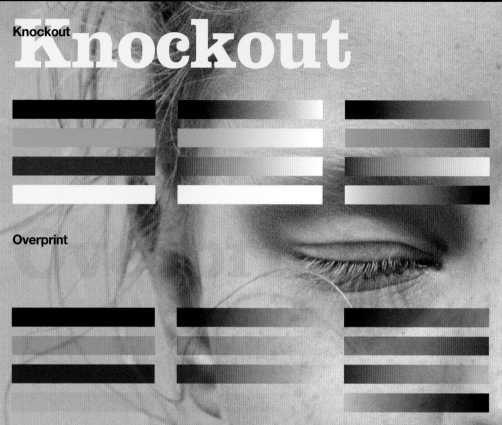

Knockout

Knockout

Overprint

It is not always obvious what the resulting difference will be between an overprint and a knockout until the job comes back from the printer – by which time it will be too late to change your mind! At the top of this page is a piece of text and a series of 12 colour bars, which were set to knockout when this book was printed. The first column contains straightforward colour blocks and you will notice the vibrancy of the four colours is retained. The second column of blocks demonstrates a linear blend to white – once the bar blends to white no image or colour is printed. The third column of blocks demonstrates a blend from one colour to another, and you will notice the transition is not interrupted.

Beneath this section, the text and series of 12 colour bars were set to overprint. Instead of vibrant colours in the first column, you will notice that the image underneath is visible. This is because the image was printed first and then the colour bars were printed on top of the image layer. The second column of blocks is again a linear blend to white. However, this time the full image underneath is revealed, giving the impression of blending between the colour bar and the image. In the third column you can clearly see the image through the colour bars, which reduces their vibrancy.

Image Mark Making

This colour image is overprinted with a series of graduated tints (ranging between 100%–10%). The middle set of tints knockout, leaving the colours preserved. The tints that overprint, particularly the lighter ones, allow more image through. As can be seen at the top, areas of the image without much colour give little interference to the colour bar, as opposed to the bottom where the interference is high.

This is a full-colour base image that has another image (of the two road signs) overprinted in black, with halftone dots at 30 LPI at a 105 degree screen angle. As you can see, this has dramatically reduced the amount of colour that shows.

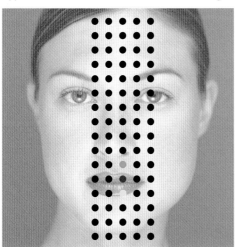

This image is a coarse yellow halftone image that incorporates halftone lines rather than dots, and is overprinted on a magenta version of the same image. This produces a distinctive, graphic feel.

This is a magenta image, which is printed at a 45 degree angle and has been overprinted with a linear blend from cyan to white.

Image Overprinting colours

Glossary

Understanding the huge variety of image types that are available, and developing the ability to incorporate them within a design, requires knowledge of the relevant technical terms and definitions used to describe them. This glossary is intended to define some of the common terminology used when dealing with images as well as some of the concepts that this terminology serves to portray. An appreciation and knowledge of these terms will facilitate a better understanding and articulation of the subject.

Some of the terms contained in the glossary refer to techniques that have been used in the production of this book, for example there is a UV spot varnish on the front cover, and pages 18–19, 22–23, 26–27 and 30–31 print with a series of special colours.